Luella Campbell Beal:

A Force to Reckon With

(Centenarian)

3rd Edition

Longevity and Health Series, Volume 1

Mary L. Beal

Inside Front Cover Commentary

"I just had to let you know how much I enjoyed the book about your mother, *Luella Campbell Beal: A Force to Reckon With*. What a wonderful job you did honoring her."

Teresa DeWitt, Syracuse, New York

"I congratulate you for putting together such a masterpiece that can serve many families in the art of unity. It is held that knowledge does not become wisdom until put into practice, Aunt Luella's life was a testimony that she was a "Lover of Humanity."

Eva Lamb, Philadelphia, Pennsylvania

Notice To Readers

The third edition of Luella Campbell Beal is being published to update information contained in the second edition. Because of the impact that it has made in the lives of many readers, consider this publication as the first volume in the Health and Longevity series. The character, Luella's primary focus during her lifetime was, God, family, community, health, and wellness. It is anticipated that the Longevity and Health Series will feature individuals who played significant roles in the lives of their families and communities.

Longevity and Health Series, Volume 1

Luella Campbell Beal - A Force to Reckon With

3rd Edition

Copyright © 2014 Mary L. Beal

All rights reserved.

ISBN: 978-1-7374348-3-2

PREFACE TO LUELLA CAMPBELL BEAL: A FORCE TO RECKON WITH 3RD EDITION

Throughout history, individuals have searched for the elusive fountain of youth. This search will probably continue until the end of time. However, for people who experienced good health and longevity, they seemed to have found the keys to the fountain of youth. Their attitude about life, their circle of friends and acquaintances, their nutritional intake throughout their lives, and their loving relationships with others, seem to display key characteristics of the fountain of youth.

A key ingredient of staying youthful and healthy is lifestyle. Luella Campbell Beal's lifestyle reflected the way of life taught to her by her parents, grandparents, aunts, uncles, her husband, ministers, and educators. Luella exhibited a great reverence for God and to God throughout her life. She strongly believed in proper nutrition, and was noted for saying, "An ounce of prevention, is worth more than a pound of cure." She took great measures to prevent diseases through cleanliness, proper rest, adequate and balanced meals, to include drinking plenty of water, and daily sunshine.

Up until ten days prior to her death, Luella spent time outdoors, attended church services, and interacted with family, friends, and neighbors. She also read something inspirational or had someone read something inspirational to her. She read a draft copy of the first edition of *Luella Campbell Beal- A Force to Reckon With*. Her comment afterwards... "That's about right." With that comment, the author realized something more needed to be added. The first edition had already been submitted to the self-publishing company when Luella Campbell Beal in the flesh transitioned into heaven. I discovered through various means some important facts and information recorded in the first edition that needed to be updated.

Many readers of the first edition commented that there appeared to be more about the character Luella than indicated in those pages. Rather than rewrite the entire first edition of this book, only corrections and editorial changes have been made for clarity and accuracy. A second book about this main character, Luella Campbell Beal, as a spiritual force to be reckon with, is published under the title, *"Help Me Cross Over from Earth to Heaven.* This book also documents Luella's transition into heaven.

Throughout Luella's life, she put her Christianity into action by how she related to others; how she raised her children; how she served God and others; and how she showed love and compassion to her family and others. Many readers of the first edition have been inspired to research and write their own personal family history after reading *Luella Campbell Beal- A Force to Reckon With.*

Many thanks to Millie Woods for being an inspiration to me in updating the first edition and writing the sequel, *Help Me Cross Over from Earth to Heaven.*

Mary L. Beal

DEDICATION

This book is dedicated to the memory of Rachel Fields and to all her descendants, living and dead. Especially, Christine Surena Olafumilayo Fasuyi, my goddaughter, who is one of Rachel Fields' many, great-great-great-great-granddaughters.

To all my nieces, nephews, and cousins with whom I have shared information about family history and family life: stay strong, and trust in the creator of the universe, God.

This project could neither have been initiated nor completed without the grace of God. Therefore, I must give Him the praise for enabling me, with the help of many others, to accomplish this awesome task. Many individuals contributed to this undertaking in a variety of ways. Some read and edited the original draft, others provided technical and editorial advice, several gave professional writing and coaching assistance, and many performed research on historical facts, while numerous others provided words of encouragement. I offer my sincere and deep appreciation for all those who contributed to this book, especially to Ruby Beal for serving as my memory bank for childhood and family experiences. I also thank all the people listed below who helped me create Luella Campbell Beal: A Force to Reckon With.

ACKNOWLEDGEMENT

Ruby Beal
Luella Beal
Jimmy Beal
James Beal
Mary Bivins
Vivian Bryant
Bertha Carnes
Dorothy Clark
Hazel Daniels
Henderson Dunn, Jr.
Avis Fasuyi
Christine Fasuyi
Francis Fasuyi
Chandra Fears
Rev. Ronrica Gordon
Brooksie Lucas Hall
Fannie Beal Harvey
Dell Ford-Jordan
Peggy King
Elizabeth Lucas
Jacqueline Beal Nickerson
Robin Porter
Bettye Roberson
Vesta Beal Shephard
Avanese Harvey Taylor
Carolyn Beal Thomas
Marshall Thomas
Molly Thomas
Merilyn Tickles
Theodore Tolbert
Barbara Walker
Marisa Wedges
Julia Mckenzie Woods
Slulami Zakade Wulah

Table of Contents	Page
PREFACE TO LUELLA CAMPBELL BEAL: A FORCE TO RECKON WITH 3RD EDITION	iv
DEDICATION	vi
ACKNOWLEDGEMENT	viii
Table of Contents	ix
Table of Figures	x
GEOGRAPHICAL HISTORICAL NOTE	xiv
Maps	xv
Figure 3: Rachel Brox Fields – Luella's Great-Grandmother	xvi
FOREWORD	xxviii
CHAPTER 1 ~ Introduction	1
CHAPTER 2 ~ Infancy and Early Childhood during World War I (1910-1919)	3
CHAPTER 3 ~ A Teenager during Prohibition 1920-1929	9
CHAPTER 4 ~ Marriage and Motherhood During the Great Depression 1930-1939	13
CHAPTER 5 ~ World War II, Motherhood and Farm Life - 1940-1949	19
CHAPTER 6 ~ Excessive Family Challenges and Losses - 1950-1959	24
CHAPTER 7 ~ Transition to City Life and Rock & Roll Music – 1950-1959	29
CHAPTER 8 ~ Civil Rights Era, College, Voting Rights - 1960-1969	37
CHAPTER 9 ~ Empty Nest – Not for Long – 1970-1979	47
CHAPTER 10 ~ Return to Parenting – Grandchildren - 1970-1979	51
CHAPTER 11 ~ Family Counselor and Hospice Caregiver 1970-1979	60

CHAPTER 12 ~ Accomplishments of the Eighties: Traveling, Community Organizing 1980- 1989	62
CHAPTER 13 ~ Refuge & Childcare, Missionary - 1990-1999	67
CHAPTER 14 ~The Sage of the Family and Community 2000-2009	74
CHAPTER 15 ~ Living Testimonies 2000-2010	81
CHAPTER 16 ~ One Hundredth Birthday Celebration February 13, 2010	88
CHAPTER 17 ~ Epilogue	92

Table of Figures	Page
Figure 1: Map Of Macon County Georgia	xiv
Figure 2: Map of Georgia	xv
Figure 3: Rachel Brox Fields – Luella's Great-Grandmother	xvi
Figure 4: Family Chart 1	xvii
Figure 5: Family Chart 2	xviii
Figure 6: Family Chart 3	xix
Figure 7: Family Chart 4	xx
Figure 8: Family Chart 5A	xxi
Figure 9: Family Chart 5B	xxii
Figure 9a: Family Chart 5B-1	xxiii
Figure 10: Family Chart 5C	xxiv
Figure 11: Family Chart 6	xxv
Figure 12: Family Chart 7	xxvi
Figure 13: Family Chart 8	xxvii
Figure 15: Luella's father and mother	3
Figure 16: Luella's Maternal Grandparents	4
Figure 16: Luella's Aunt whom she was named to honor	5
Figure 17: Luella's two oldest sisters, Josephine (left) Julia(right)	7
Figure 18: Luella's Aunt Victoria "Vic"	8
Figure 19: Photo of Luella as a young lady	11
Figure 20: Luella's in-laws Left	12
Figure 21: Luella's Marriage Certificate	13
Figure 22: Wash Pot	16
Figure 23: Rub Board	16
Figure 24: Galvanized Wash Tub	16
Figure 25: Luella's brother-in-Law Paten	18

Figure 26: Luella's Father-in-law and step-mother-in-law	21
Figure 27: Luella's Family	23
Figure 28: Newspaper Clipping from 1958	30
Figure 29: The Lord Will Make A Way Somehow	41
Figure 29a: Luella's Voter Registration	42
Figure 30: Luella's home was built in 1970	45
Figure 31: Great-grandchildren Ilene, Jerry, Emmanuel, &	46
Figure 32: Luella (right) with youngest sister, and cousin, James Fields	48
Figure 33: Luella's youngest daughter's wedding	50
Figure 34: Luella's two oldest brothers	52
Figure 35: James "Happy", wife Patience	55
Figure 36: Luella dancing with a hula hoop	56
Figure 37: Alexander Campbell	56
Figure 38: Richard Campbell	57
Figure 39: Charlie Campbell	57
Figure 40: Eula Campbell McKenzie	58
Figure 41: Brooksie Campbell Lucas	58
Figure 42: Seabright Seay Wiggins	59
Figure 43: Lucille Hargrove Dixon	59
Figure 44: Luella at granddaughter's wedding in 1984,	64
Figure 45: Luella's youngest granddaughter's high school	68
Figure 46: Luella with two of her nieces, Rena and Vesta	69
Figure 47: Luella's oldest great-granddaughter high school	70
Figure 48: Luella's Nigerian Family 1	71
Figure 49: Luella's great-grandson high school	71

graduation	
Figure 50: Macedonia Baptist Church (founded in 1870)	73
Figure 51: Luella's oldest great-granddaughter wedding	78
Figure 52: Family picture taken at oldest son's 75th	79
Figure 53: Five generations that attended the 2009 Fields	80
Figure 54: Luella with her five living children on her 100th Birthday	88
Figure 55: Cake designed and made by Luella's brother-in-law,	88
Figure 56: Birthday wishes from The White House	89
Figure 57: Proclamation for Luella Campbell Beal by Cordele, GA	91
Figure 58: Proclamation of Luella Campbell Beal Day Crisp County	92
Figure 59: Thank You Card from Luella	93
Figure 60: A Tribute to my mom on her Ninetieth Birthday	94
Figure 61: Living Testimony by	95
Figure 62: Matthew 6:19-34 (KJV)	98

GEOGRAPHICAL HISTORICAL NOTE

Dooly County was created by an act of the Georgia General Assembly on May 15, 1821. It was one of the original land lot counties created from land ceded from the Creek Nation (Native Americans).

The entire county of Crisp and parts of Macon, Pulaski, Turner, Wilcox, and Worth counties were formed from Dooly's original borders. Macon County was created in 1837 from Houston ("house-ton") and Marion counties, effective December 14 of that year. Macon County was named for Nathaniel Macon of North Carolina who served in the U.S. Congress for 37 years and ran for U.S. vice-president.

According to oral family history and the United States Census Bureau, Luella's maternal great-grandmother was also from North Carolina; and her maternal great-grandfather was born in Virginia. It appears that her maternal grandfather also had family roots in North Carolina. Luella's paternal grandparents came to Georgia from South Carolina.

More research must be completed to determine if there was any linkage between those families in Virginia, North Carolina, and South Carolina.

Maps

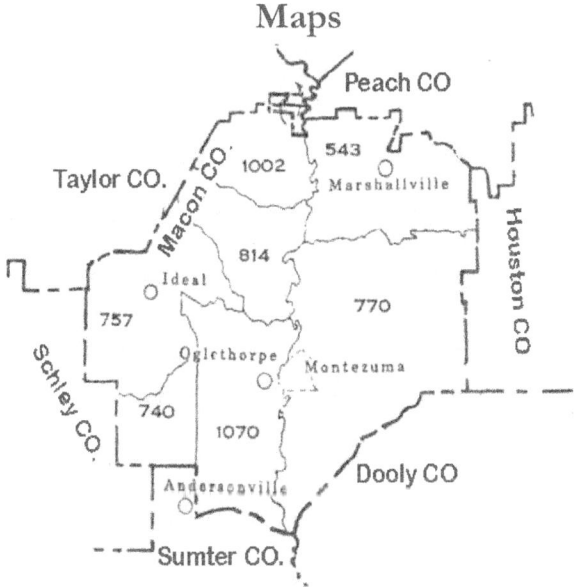

Figure 1: Map of Macon County Georgia

Figure 2: Map of Georgia

Figure 3: Rachel Mnu Fields – Luella's Great-Grandmother

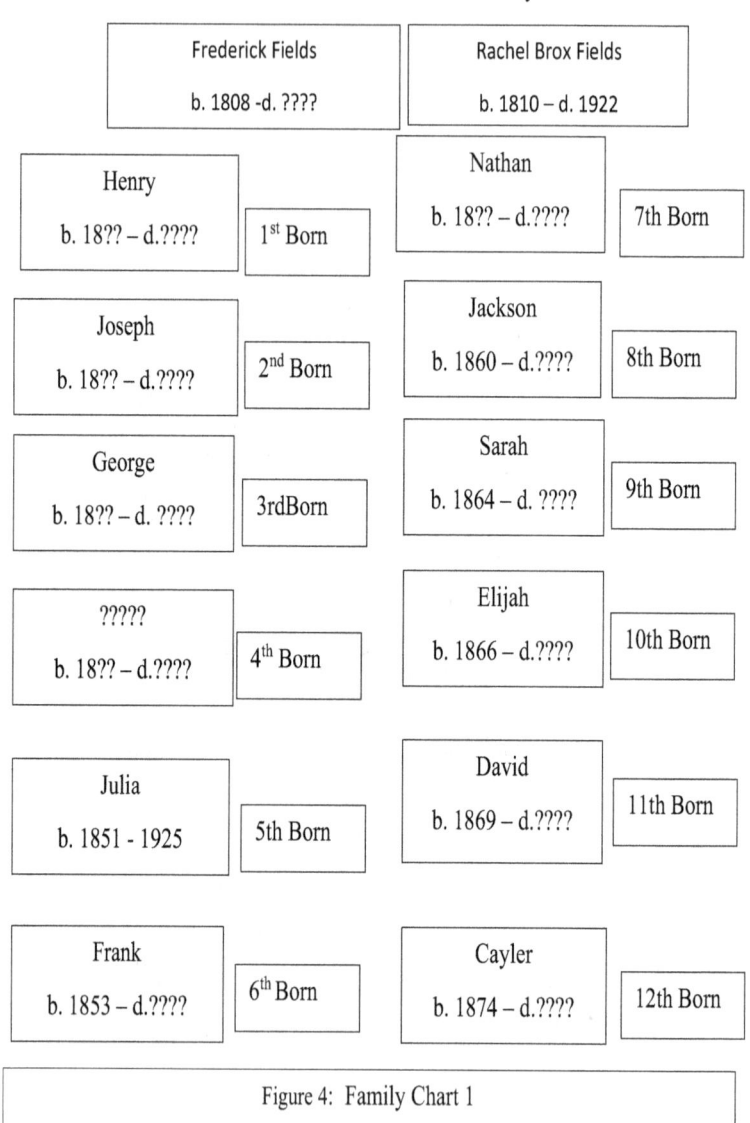

Figure 4: Family Chart 1

xviii

Abraham Massey & Julia Fields' Family

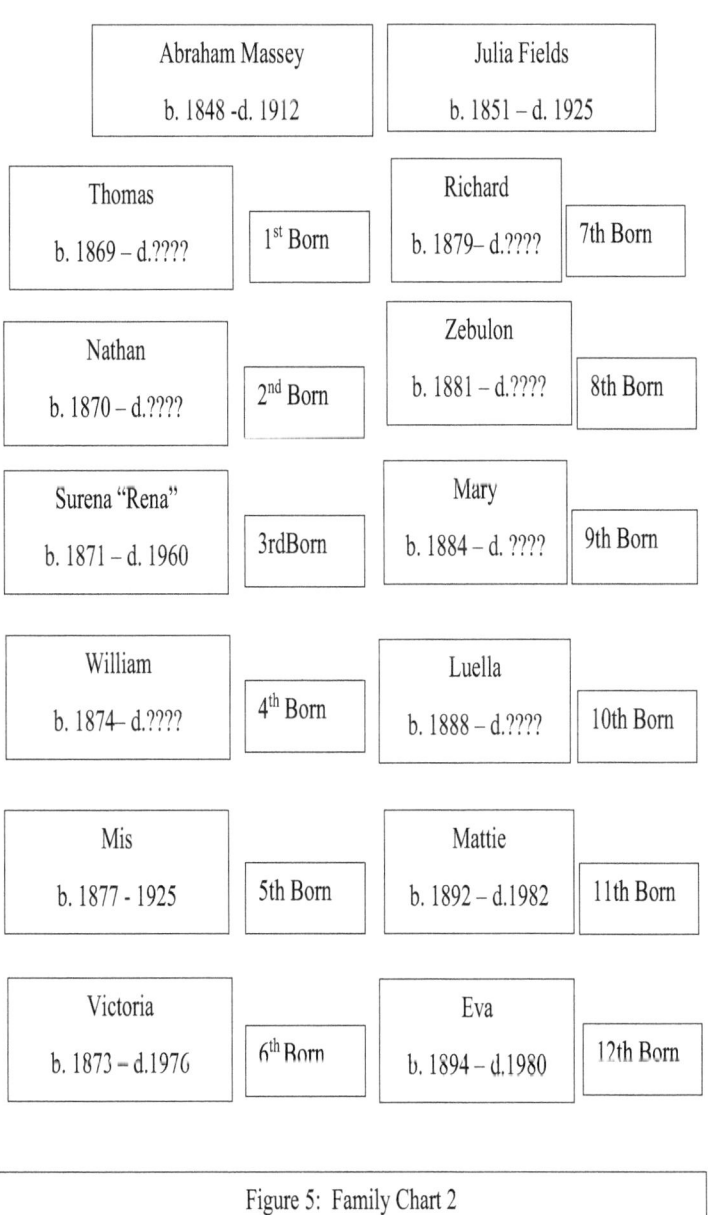

Figure 5: Family Chart 2

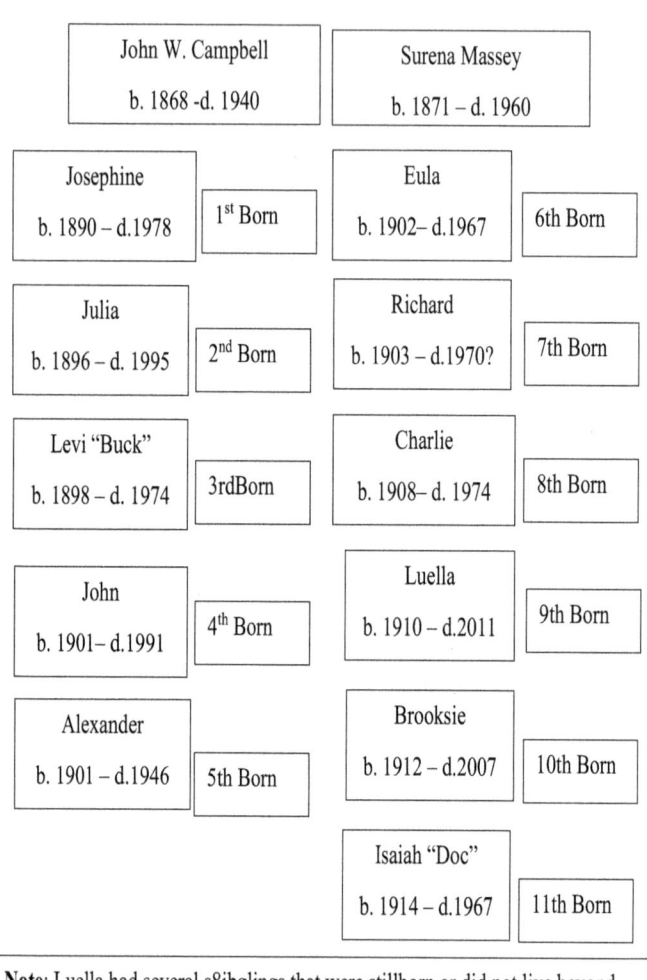

Note: Luella had several s8ibglings that were stillborn or did not live beyond infancy. Also note that only one of Luella's siblings who reached maturity preceded their mother in death

Figure 6: Family Chart 3

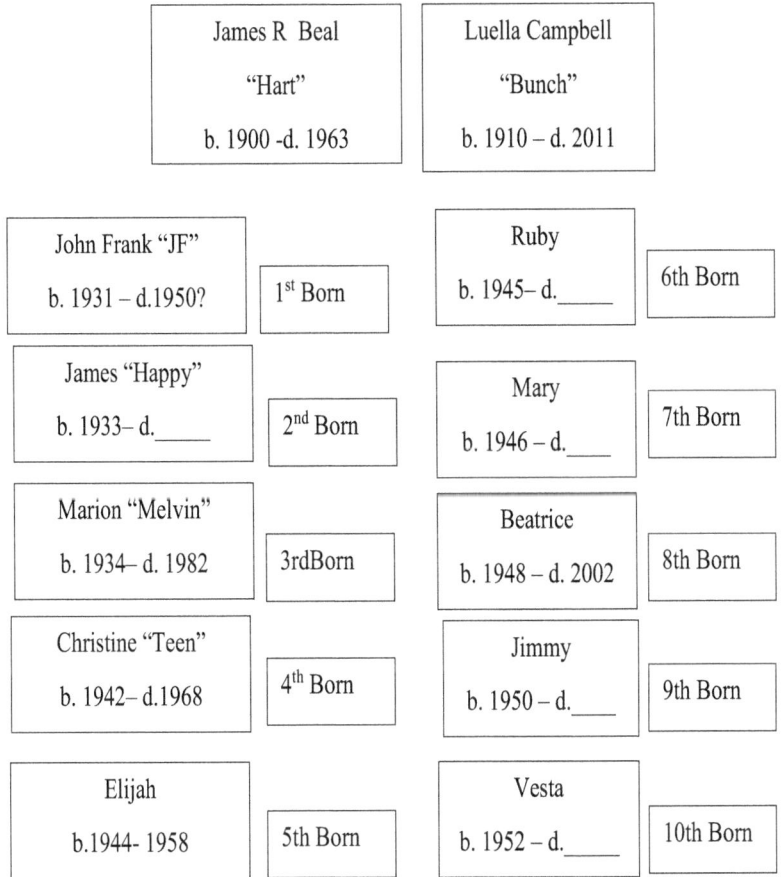

Figure 7: Family Chart 4

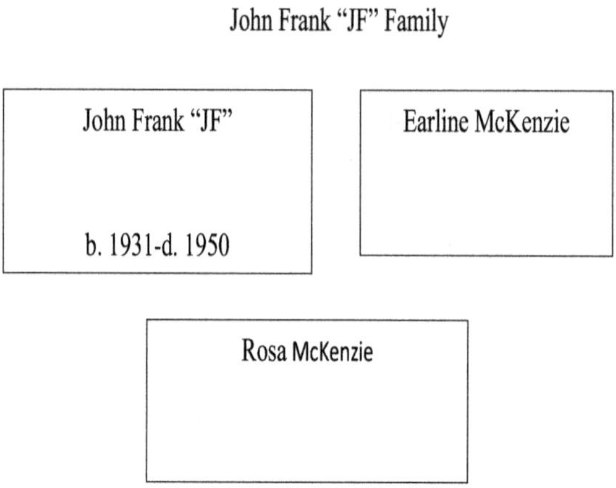

John Frank "JF" Family

| John Frank "JF"

b. 1931-d. 1950 |

| Earline McKenzie |

| Rosa McKenzie |

Figure 8: Family Chart 5A

James "Happy" & Patience's Family

| James Beal "Happy" b. 1933 - d. _____ | Patience Tolbert b. 1935 – d. 1972 |

Joseph b. 1954 – d. 1954?	1st Born
Fannie b. ____ – d. ____	2nd Born
James b. ____ – d. ____	3rd Born
Bertha b. ____ – d. ____	4th Born
Alvin b. ____ – d. ____	5th Born
Nathaniel b. ____ – d. ____	6th Born

Avis b. ____ 5 – d. ____	7th Born
Donald b. ____ – d. ____	8th Born
Herman b. ____ – d. ____	9th Born
Robert b. ____ – d. ____	10th Born
Scottye b. ____ –	11th Born
Jacqueline b. ____ –	12th Born

Figure 9: Family Chart 5B

James "Happy" Other Family

James Beal
"Happy"
b. 1933 -d. _____

Chris Brown
b. _____ – d. _____

Figure 9a: Family Chart 5B-1

Beatrice's Family

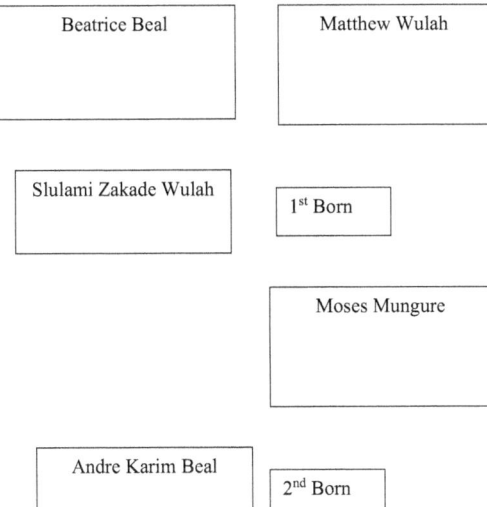

Figure 10: Family Chart 5C

Luella &n James' Great-Grandchildren

Mario	Alvin	Avanese
Joseph	Ilene	Christopher
Kelvin	Jeremiah	Deza
Emmanuel	Rantonio	Nazirah
Christine	Jaleel	Aquil
Destiny	Skyla	Robert, Jr
Scottye, Jr	JreShaun Luell	Charles
Jimmy	Anthony	Hiram
Hillary	Alexandria	Llondyn

Figure 11: Family Chart 6

Luella & James' Great-Great-Grandchildren

Khaliyah	Vanessa	Patience
Everett	Charleston	Carolina
Aisha	Samuel	Kiyana
Micah	DeMari	Kenneth
JoMari	Leona	Santos

Figure 12: Family Chart 7

Luella & James' Great-Great-Great-Grandchildren

Antonio	Texiciahna	Makayla
Arielle	Sharema	Jimmy
Shatana	Adriana	

Figure 13: Family Chart 8

xxviii

FOREWORD
By
Gloria Donaldson, Founder and Executive Director,
WordPower Christian Education Outreach

Luella Campbell Beal: A Force to Reckon With is an important biographical archive that manifests enduring love and family unity as personified in Luella Beal. Heartwarming and compelling, this is an intimate, true story about the sacrifices, wisdom, innate persuasion, and authority of a black matriarchal icon in the South.

It speaks of one born not long after the Emancipation Proclamation who would one day cast her vote in favor of America's first African American President. The book speaks volumes about this genuine Christian sojourner, wife, mother, grandmother, aunt, neighbor, and friend. In between the lines and in unspoken words, it reveals a web of tremendous affection, friendship and respect forged between a cherished, highly esteemed mother and her devoted daughter, Mary Beal. What a literary masterpiece! It illustrates that charity really does begin at home and spreads abroad. This book packs loads of inspiration for every family.

CHAPTER 1 ~ Introduction

In the winter of 1910, a special girl was born in a small rural town in Georgia. The town was Montezuma which is noted for its Elberta peaches. Her parents, John and Surena Campbell, named her Luella. During that time, it was customary for Black families to name their children in honor of other individuals, especially family members and close friends. Luella was named in honor of one of her mother's sister, Luella Massey Salmon.

Local churches were the hub for social interaction. Luella's family was no different and participated in church-sponsored activities. Because there were no public schools for Black children, Luella attended church-related schools. She was taught her ABC's and how to read and pray, all in the House of the Lord!

As Luella grew and developed into a mature lady, she continued to participate in church functions. She began to take an active interest in social functions, because she had caught the eye of a certain handsome young man. It was at one of the church's social functions where Luella was swept off her feet by Mr. James Beal. Soon thereafter, the church bells trumpeted following their nuptial ceremony.

Luella joined Macedonia Baptist Church in the Drayton Community (located near Vienna, GA), where James and other members of the Beal family were members. Until her death, at the age of one hundred one, Miss Luella attended Macedonia, and was the oldest living member of that flock. Many of the current congregants are direct descendants of the church's founders. Since 1870, these families have worshipped, prayed, wept, and played together.

Luella firmly believed that to truly serve God, one must serve mankind. Putting her faith into action, Luella joined the Macedonia Baptist Church's "Missionary Board." As a Christian, Luella taught her children that one enters church to worship and departs to serve.

Luella raised ten children and a host of grandchildren; she taught all of them to put God first in their lives. She taught each of her ten children the Lord's Prayer at a very early age. Luella ensured that her children and grandchildren attended Sunday school and church regularly. Luella encouraged her children to read the Bible and she reinforced her teaching by requiring each child to recite a verse from the Bible at each meal during the blessing of the food. At the age of one hundred, she recited the Lord's Prayer before she retired to bed each night.

The church, as the center of life in the community, was used to communicate with residents by the ringing of church bells. The different bell tones communicated specific messages. The death of a resident was denoted by a slow "bong", "bong", "bong" bell tone. A disaster was communicated by a rapid pull on the church bell cord that generated "bing", "bing", "bing", a brighter sound. The start of church service was indicated by a steady pull on the church's bell cord. Luella heard many church bells ring during her lifetime.

Luella encountered many challenges and obstacles during her one hundred one years of living. Her husband and five of their beloved children and one grandchild preceded her in death. She was the last to leave this earth of twelve siblings. Luella's husband died and left her a widow to raise six children between the ages of nine and twenty. The oldest of the six children had a handicap and a life-threatening medical condition. Luella served as caregiver for a daughter, two brothers, one sister-in-law and one aunt. Her faith in God was displayed in her daily living.

Luella's faith in God was evident by her prayers, and her Christian works. She served her family, her church, her neighbors, and her community for more than eighty years with a joyful heart. God rewarded her on earth in tangible and intangible ways. Her intangible rewards are not visible to the naked eye.

Luella's earthly rewards (tangible) include her home, which was constructed under her supervision when she was 60 years of age. She resided there until her death at one hundred and one years. Other tangible rewards were five living children and a host of other descendants, all of whom are part of her legacy.

As for her intangible rewards, none of her direct descendants were homeless or incarcerated and practically everyone participates in church and/or public service. Her most valuable intangible reward is the receipt of one of God's promises – longevity – ONE HUNDRED PLUS YEARS OF LIVING AN ABUNDANT LIFE.

"For all our days are passed away in the wrath, we spend our years as a tale that is told. The days of our years are three score years and ten and if by reason of strength they be fourscore years, yet is there strength labour and sorrow, for it is soon cut off, and we fly away. Who knoweth the power of thine anger? Even according to thy fear, so is thy wrath. So, teach us to number our days, that we may apply our hearts with wisdom" (KJV, Psalms 90:9-10). Luella's tale shows that she was a force to reckon with for ten decades.

CHAPTER 2 ~ Infancy and Early Childhood during World War I *(1910-1919)*

Children and parents share an inseparable bond because of bloodline and life itself. Often, bonds between mothers and children appear to be more evident than bonds between father and children. Aristotle stated, "This is the reason why mothers are more devoted to their children than fathers: it is that they suffer more in giving them birth and are more certain that they are their own."

On a very cold Sunday morning in a small South Georgia town, Rena Campbell's water broke (she went into labor). Rena's mother, Julia, was there by her side to catch the baby girl. Rena's husband, John, had earlier added logs to the fire in the fireplace to keep his wife and newborn baby warm.

As was the customary practice, Julia loudly announced the baby's gender by stating, "It's a girl!" Julia said to Rena, "Let's name her in honor of your sister, and my daughter Luella."

The newborn baby girl, Luella, had one of the most experienced midwives in the town to assist her entry into the world. One of Luella's first cousins said about their grandmother Julia, "She really could catch some babies." Julia was in her mid-sixties and still very active when Luella was born.

Figure 14. Luella's father and mother

John and Surena

Baby Luella was blessed by longevity in parents, grandparents, and great-grandparents. Her great-grandmother, Rachel, Julia's mother, was alive and active when Baby Luella was born. Her maternal grandmother, Julia lived to almost ninety years of age and her maternal great-grandmother lived for more than one hundred years.

Figure 15: Luella's Maternal Grandparents

Abraham & Julia Fields Massey

Luella's tale began on a cold day on the second Sunday in February 1910. However, her genetic tale began thousands of years earlier. According to the *Macon County Citizen*, the topic for the Sunday school lesson on that date was "Worldliness and Trust." The scripture for that lesson was Matthew 6:19-34. In many ways these verses provided prophetic meaning for Luella's future life. By relating Luella's living testimony, her strengths, labors, sorrows, happiness, love, wisdom, humor, and unwavering courage this prophetic 'force to reckon with' will be revealed.

Frederick Fields moved his family to west central Georgia on the eve of the Civil War during the mid-1800s. Since the 1860s, the family roots have been planted in and around Macon County, Georgia. Although many family members physically left the area during the great migration (1915 – 1940) from fields in the south to factories in the north, their hearts and memories remained.

Older family members usually remained in the South and they either lived on their own or resided with other family members. The Fields, Massey and Campbell clans possessed many survival skills and vocations since their heritage included African, Native American, and European lineages. The Fields were categorized as mulattoes in early U. S. Census schedules.

Luella's paternal grandfather Alexander Campbell, Sr. was a farmer and a minister of the Gospel. As a minister, he performed many marriages, preached many sermons, and delivered the eulogy for many funerals. One of his in-laws by marriage was Rev. M. C. Fields, happened to be one of Luella's cousins. These two elderly family members provided much of the spiritual foundation that shaped the lives of Luella and her siblings. Julia Fields Massey, in addition to being a mid-wife was taught by her mother, Rachel Fields, how to cook and maintain a household. Luella's bloodline was derived from all these families plus many other unknown ones. Therefore, her early childhood included interaction with both her maternal and paternal ancestors with a variety of habits and customs common to African, European, and Native American heritages. At the time of Luella's birth, both her maternal and paternal grandmothers and grandfathers were alive. Several great aunts and uncles were also alive; therefore, Luella was ingrained with the philosophy of respecting and honoring one's elders.

Figure 16: Luella's Aunt whom she was named to honor.

John and Surena were loving parents who feared God and displayed compassion for their neighbors and friends. Both were born less than a decade after the Civil War and after the eradication of slavery in the United States of America. Therefore, her parents did not experience the ravages of war or human bondage (slavery).

John was a farmer on the banks of the Flint River. Surena was an excellent cook and housewife. Surena made quilts that signified people and unity. At the time of Luella's birth, government officials had not implemented universal issuance of birth certificates. Therefore, Luella does not possess a regular birth certificate.

During that time, it was common practice for families to record births, deaths, and marriages in the family Bible in the genealogy section. Another source that documented her birth was the U. S. Census Bureau decennial census taken in 1910. Census Day in 1910 was the first day of April.

Luella Campbell was the third youngest of eleven children who survived infancy. She had three older sisters, Josephine, Julia, and Eula. There were five older brothers, Levi (Buck), John, Alex, Richard, and Charlie. Her youngest sister, Brooksie, was two and one-half years younger and her youngest brother, Isaiah (Doc) Campbell was born four years later Luella's birthday. The family resided in the Traveler's Rest Community.

John and Surena received assistance from many other family members in raising Luella. These family members included her maternal grandmother, Julia; maternal great-grandmother, Rachel; and a host of aunts, uncles, great-uncles, older siblings, and close neighbors who provided guidance. All of them plus others helped to develop Luella's strength of character that made her a strong force to reckon with in later life.

A White citizen of Macon County murdered Luella's maternal grandfather, Abraham (Abe), over an issue pertaining to land and crops, two years, and six months after her birth. Therefore, she did not have an opportunity to develop a long-term meaningful relationship with her maternal grandfather. Luella was able to establish a relationship with her maternal grandmother, Julia, and her maternal great-grandmother Rachel. Luella remembered her great-grandmother and always fondly recounted to her children that when she was twelve years old, her great-grandmother Rachel was one hundred and twelve.

Surena, Luella's mother, had five sisters and five brothers. The sisters were Victoria (Vic), Rosabelle, Luella, Mattie, and Eva. Surena's brothers' names were William (Billy), Thomas, Abraham, Richard, and Zebulon.

Vic married and moved to Savannah, Georgia. Rosabelle married and moved to Valdosta, Georgia. Luella married and remained in Macon County, and Mattie married and moved to the adjacent Dooly County. Eva married Jerry Moran who later had her committed to the State of Georgia Asylum for the Insane. Surena's brothers did not maintain constant contact with the family like her sisters did; however, Luella received knowledge of her uncles and her cousins through her mother and older siblings. Luella's oldest and youngest maternal aunts played a large role in her life in later years.

Josephine, Luella's oldest sister, was almost twenty years old when she was born. Therefore, before Luella became old enough to attend school, her oldest sister Josephine had married and given birth to her oldest child, a daughter named Vesta. Vesta not only became one of Luella's childhood playmates, but a lifetime friend. Luella's second oldest sister, Julia was fourteen years older and became a schoolteacher. Luella prospered from having older siblings. She loved to read, and her older brothers would purchase books, magazines, and newspapers for her.

Luella forged a close bond with all her siblings; however, she

Figure 17: Luella's two oldest sisters, Josephine (left) Julia(right)

appeared to have the closet bond with her youngest sister Brooksie and her oldest brother, fondly called 'Buck'. Buck is the only person who called her by a nickname. Buck gave her the nickname 'Bunch' because he said that practically every time, he visited his parents when Luella was a youngster, she would be seen with a bunch of peanuts.

Her second youngest brother Charlie was her childhood nemesis. Charlie taught her how to shoot marbles, which was not a very ladylike game. He taught her how to climb trees and shoot a shotgun. Luella's maternal family attended Traveler's Rest Methodist and Traveler's Rest Baptist Churches. She also attended Mount Olive Baptist Church in Dooly County, Georgia with her father. John Campbell and one of his brothers helped build Mount Olive Baptist Church. Luella was baptized around the age of ten in Traveler's Rest Creek. Traveler's Rest, Shade Arnold, Mount Olive and Macedonia Baptist Churches are all within a thirty-mile radius of each other.

Luella attended school at Traveler's Rest, Shade Arnold, and

Macedonia Baptist Church Schools. She became an avid reader. She completed her primary education in Macon County Schools. During the 1920's, the family moved to Dooly County and Luella continued her education. Mandatory education for children between the ages of six and sixteen began during the 1920s.

Therefore, Luella's law-abiding parents ensured that she attended school. Luella loved school and wanted to become a teacher like one of her older sisters and one of her uncles.

Luella's early life was spent attending church and school, performing chores around the farm, and playing with siblings, cousins, and neighbors. Luella also performed household chores and learned the art of quilt making. Some of her favorite first cousins were Little Zeb, Seabright, and Ollie May. In addition to her first cousins, Luella's youngest sister, Brooksie, her two youngest brothers, Charlie, and Isaiah (Doc), and her oldest niece, Vesta, were also her playmates.

Figure 18: Luella's Aunt Victoria "Vic"

CHAPTER 3 ~ A Teenager during Prohibition 1920-1929

Luella was only ten years old in 1920 when the U. S. Congress passed voting rights legislation for women. She became a teenager during the "Roaring Twenties." During that timeframe rural electrification had not come to Macon and Dooly Counties in Georgia. Therefore, Luella studied and read by kerosene lanterns and candlelight. She deeply wanted to attend college, but her parents could not afford to send her. However, she received the highest level of education available locally during that time. She taught school for lower grades in Dooly County, like her older sisters did in Macon County.

By then, Luella's parents had reached fifty to sixty years of age. All her older siblings had married and moved away to different towns, cities, and states while Luella remained on the farm and assisted her parents with household and farm chores. Luella learned how to make quilts and soap; how to plant and harvest fruits and vegetables; and to milk cows. She also learned how to raise chickens. Luella assisted her father with cultivation and harvesting of farm crops.

She learned how to wash and assisted her mother in laundering household linen and family members' clothes. There were seven steps in performing household laundry tasks. The first step involved separating white laundry items from darker items. The second step was placing the white items in a cast iron vessel and boiling them with lye soap. In the third step, clothes were removed from the boiling water and placed in the first of three galvanized number three wash tubs. In the first tub, Luella would scrub extra soiled spots on a rub board. The soapy water was squeezed out, item by item, and placed in the second galvanized tub as the first rinse. The same process was repeated in the third galvanized tub, which usually was the final rinse. Laundry items were fastened on rows and rows of clotheslines in the fifth step. The sixth step in preparing the family laundry was taking the clothes off the line and ironing them. The laundry process was not complete until clothes were ironed and placed in an assigned storage area.

The Campbell's did not have running water. They retrieved their water supply from a well. It had to be drawn one bucket at a time. Therefore, it took the better part of a whole day to perform household laundry tasks. Typically, Monday was "Wash Day" in most households. Basically, all farm households in west central Georgia used wells to provide water for all their needs during the 1920s.

When two of Luella's older brothers, Richard, and Charlie, left home and married, she assisted her father in caring for the family's livestock and retrieved firewood for cooking and heating. Luella fed the hogs, took cows out to pasture, milked the cows twice a day and pitched hay to the mules. She also learned to churn milk and make fresh butter by hand. She gathered eggs from the henhouse. During the Fall of the year, Luella assisted her parents with special duties required during hog slaughtering. She learned how to salt down specific parts of hog meat and how to prepare stews and sausages from other parts of the hog, and how to slaughter and clean chickens, turkeys, and rabbits.

On various occasions, Luella was allowed to visit and spend nights and weekends with her Aunt Luella in Montezuma and her cousins in Byromville, Dooling, and Lilly, Georgia. Luella developed close friendships with several students at school. Two of them became life-long friends and one of them became her sister-in-law. They were Mrs. Lucille Hargrove Dixon and Mrs. Mary Alice Beal Hightower. Luella did on occasions socialize by attending house parties. She recalled that once while attending a house party, the roof fell in. The church also held socials for young adults. These events included refreshments, gospel music and many conversations.

Romantic Love

Mary Alice introduced Luella to one of her older brothers, James Robert Beal, at a church social during the late part of the 1920s. James was one of Frank and Mary Beal's older sons. He had recently returned home from years of absence from the family because of his wanderlust. James left home before he reached the age of seventeen. He returned home because of an injury he received while working on the railroad system.

James courted Luella in the parlor or on the front porch of Luella's home. Their courtship lasted for several months, and they were married on December 27, 1930. Luella probably feared becoming a spinster because her youngest sister, Brooksie married before she did. Reverend D. E. Bryant of Macedonia Baptist Church in Drayton, Georgia performed the marriage ceremony. James was thirty years of age and Luella was ten years his junior when they married. James and Luella had many common interests, and both loved the Lord.

They also shared a mutual love for family and friends. Luella and James lived most of their married life near his family members. Over the years, Luella became an integral part of the Beal family. She was able to blend into the large family because of the way she was raised and because of her respect for herself and her elders. She had an amicable relationship with both her father-in-law and her mother-in-law.

Luella and James showed their respect and honored both sets of parents by naming their first born in honor of both grandfathers. Their first-born child's name was John Frank. They shared many happy years and had been married for almost thirty-three years prior to his untimely death. It was not a surprise that Luella interacted with her in-laws in such a highly amicable manner. James' youngest sister, Mary Alice, remained a close companion of Luella's throughout her lifetime. Luella also became very close friends with her husband's two youngest brothers, Willie Lee and Paten and their wives.

Figure 19: Photo of Luella as a young lady

Figure 20: Luella's in-laws Left.

Magnolia Beal, Shade & Lelia Beal Haddock, and their granddaughter Melba Haddock; Right: Eva Beal Evans

CHAPTER 4 ~ Marriage and Motherhood During the Great Depression 1930-1939

Marriage and motherhood during the Great Depression between the years of 1930-1939 were very challenging for Luella. However, she was able to withstand these hardships because of her training and experience passed down from her parents. During the decade of the 1930s, Luella gave birth to three children, all sons. They survived the hardships encountered by many families during the Great Depression because of hard work, family unity and by maintaining faith in God. Even though the Beal families were able to maintain healthy diets during the Depression years, they were like the rest of the population when it came to the rationing of supplies and commodities.

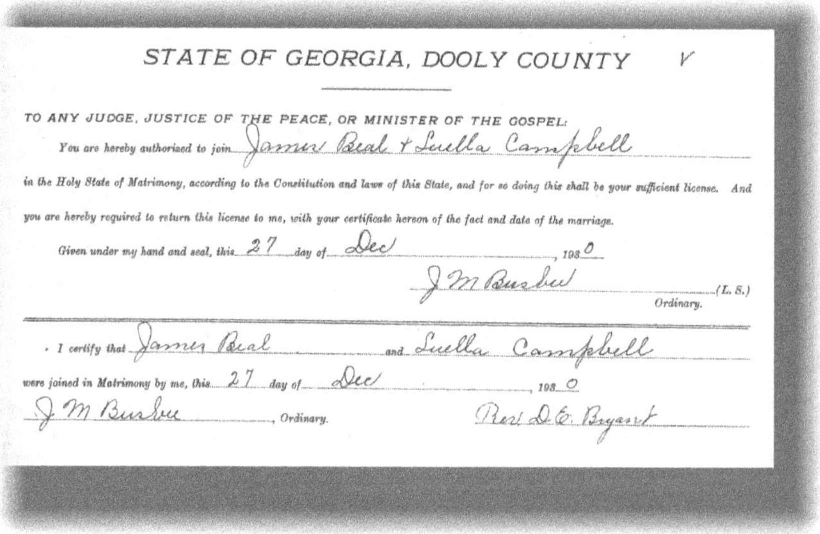

STATE OF GEORGIA, DOOLY COUNTY

TO ANY JUDGE, JUSTICE OF THE PEACE, OR MINISTER OF THE GOSPEL:

You are hereby authorized to join James Beal + Luella Campbell

in the Holy State of Matrimony, according to the Constitution and laws of this State, and for so doing this shall be your sufficient license. And you are hereby required to return this license to me, with your certificate hereon of the fact and date of the marriage.

Given under my hand and seal, this 27 *day of* Dec, 1930

J M Busbee (L. S.)
Ordinary.

I certify that James Beal *and* Luella Campbell *were joined in Matrimony by me, this* 27 *day of* Dec, 1930

J M Busbee, *Ordinary.*

Rev D. E. Bryant

Figure 21: Luella's Marriage Certificate

They lived on the Old Leonard Estate which was rented by Luella's in-laws. The Old Leonard Estate is located about eight miles northwest of Cordele, Georgia, the Watermelon Capital of the World, where she lived with her family and in-laws for one quarter of a century. Her in-laws included her father-in-law, two sisters-in-law and their husbands and one brother-in-law and his wife. It should be explained that her brother-in-law, Paten, his first wife died very young, and he later remarried. Luella's mother-in-law died in 1933 within the first three years of her marriage. Her sister-in-law, Leila, who also lived on the farm, gave birth to three children who were about the same ages as Luella's and James' three older children.

Therefore, their lives became interwoven because of their children, school, church, work, and holiday festivities in which they all participated. Everyone also participated in the planting and harvesting of crops.

Each household had acreage allotted for their own personal use. They individually decided on which crops they would plant each year. Usually, everyone planted cotton, watermelon, cantaloupes, peanuts, and corn. They would alternate bell peppers, tomatoes, cucumbers, peas, butterbeans, and sweet potatoes. There were a variety of pecan trees on the farm. There also were fig, peach, pomegranate, pear, and plum trees located at almost every household. Blackberries and blueberries grew wild in the forest areas on the farm.

Luella maintained a vegetable garden that produced food for her family's household consumption. She routinely planted spring, summer and fall gardens. Luella planted collards, turnip greens, squash, okra, butterbeans, snap beans, onions, beets, and tomatoes. Luella would manually water plants in the vegetable garden.

All the wives actively participated in canning fruits and vegetables during spring, summer and fall months. Sometimes, they would prepare their fruits and vegetables then travel to the adjacent town to the canning factory to preserve their fruits and vegetables. Other times, they would remain at home and preserve their fruits and vegetables in their own kitchens with the aid of pressure cookers. Their children would participate by shelling peas and butterbeans or by peeling tomatoes, peaches, and pears. The children would also help by sterilizing canning jars. Over the years, Mama was awarded many ribbons for her canned goods entered in competition at the county fair.

Several of Mama's children remembered when their house burned in the spring of 1954 and recalled hearing sounds that closely related to machine guns' firing. The sounds were produced when the hot flames heated the cold canned fruit and vegetable jars and caused an explosion.

During the late fall and winter months, the women spent a lot of time at the quilting horse making quilts. A quilting horse is a wooden frame with four legs, two short wooden slats on each end, and two long wooden poles that fit in slots on the left and right sides of the frame. The frame allowed quilters to sit and stitch their patches and designs then roll the completed sections out of sight until the whole quilt was completed.

The women on the farm would harvest small, dried reed-like wild plants to make brooms for the house. They would enter the forest area to cut a long evergreen spindle like plant for use as a broom to sweep the yards. Sweeping the yards was basically a chore performed on Saturday by older children or females on the farm.

There were many chores reserved for children, including shelling dried corn for chicken feed, and carrying firewood from the woodpile, either to the kitchen for the wood-burning stove or to the various fireplaces in the homes. Children would feed the livestock by pitching hay or placing corn and water in the troughs. Chores reserved for older children included taking cows out to pasture, milking cows, drawing water from the well; helping wash and hang laundry on the clothesline; and pitching hay to livestock. Older children also assisted with taking care of younger siblings. Luella always planted vegetable and flower gardens. She learned the medicinal properties of many flowers and herbs from her parents and grandparents. She and her husband raised chickens, turkeys, and hogs. They always kept at least one milk cow, churned their own butter, and made their own sugar cane syrup.

James and Luella had a very large smokehouse where salted pork products were stored. They also stored some canned fruits in the smokehouse. Luella was a great homemaker. Each household had a sewing machine, and the wives made accessories for the home and clothes for family members. Luella also made soap from animal fat products and lye. She was very industrious; she used flour sacks to make pillowcases, aprons, and clothes for her daughters.

Both James and Luella loved to read. There were always a Bible, a Sunday school book, and several newspapers in the home. James routinely purchased two separate weekly Black newspapers: <u>The Chicago Defender</u> and <u>The Pittsburgh Courier</u>.

The radio was the family's primary source of current, local, and national news as well as sports and entertainment. The family listened to such shows as Amos and Andy, professional baseball games, boxing, as well as various music and news programs. The family listened to the commentator of the Joe Louis fight when he won the title from Max Spelling. Their favorite radio program on Saturday nights was Randy's Record Mart in Nashville, Tennessee. Both James and Luella loved to listen to gospel music. On Sunday mornings, the family would listen to local gospel radio programs during breakfast preparation. They also listened to gospel programs on WLAC radio broadcast from Nashville, Tennessee.

James and Luella both possessed a good sense of humor and Luella displayed quick wit. Beal family lore states that James received an injury to his head years earlier by clowning on top of a moving train. Sometimes, Luella would teasingly comment to an individual, "You must forgive Jumbo for he has a plate in his head." "Jumbo" was Luella's nickname for her husband, James, and he would often retort, "I am crazy in love with that woman." They would often pass a special touch or wink between each other.

Luella's household garden contained a variety of vegetables: tomatoes, corn, snap beans, bell peppers, peas, butterbeans, squash, sweet potatoes, and okra. Luella performed a lot of manual labor because during her entire residence on the Old Leonard Estate she did not have indoor running water. The water system on the Old Leonard Estate was only a deep Artesian well. Water was drawn by submerging a bucket on a rope down into a deep crevice until it filled with water. The bucket held only one gallon of water.

Figure 22: Wash Pot

Figure 23: Rub Board

There were no indoor plumbing facilities or a central heating and cooling system. Luella prepared all the family meals on a wood-burning stove. She canned and preserved most of her jams and jellies by using the wood-burning stove. On Mondays, "wash day," as she had been trained by her mother, Luella drew many buckets of water and filled three galvanized tubs. She also used a cast iron pot to boil the dirt and germs out of clothes as she had been taught.

Luella hung rows and rows of clothes on clothesline with clothes pins to prevent them from falling to the ground. The process for cleaning laundry was very labor intensive; therefore, extra precaution was taken to prevent cleaned clothes from touching the ground. During thunderstorms and hurricane seasons, there were often occasions when Luella had to rush to take laundry in off clotheslines or get clothes washed and dried before it rained.

Figure 24: Galvanized Wash Tub

During non-planting and non-harvesting seasons, Luella would pack up her children and board the train to visit various family members throughout Georgia and Florida. On rare occasions, she would travel by train to Atlanta and her oldest brother would drive them to Chattanooga to visit their sister, Julia. She would visit those family members in the surrounding commuting area by auto. Her husband and in-laws always owned cars and trucks. Her father-in-law was very partial to the Packard automobile and her husband, and his youngest brother showed partiality to Chevrolet vehicles. Luella mentioned that her father was the owner of the first Cadillac automobile in Macon County.

Trucks were used for multiple purposes. Their primary use was to transport fruits and vegetables to the Farmer's Market in Cordele. However, on Sundays they became utility vehicles for transportation to take children and adults to Sunday school and church in the Drayton community.

Trucks were the most efficient form of transportation since several portable benches were placed on the bed of the truck and more people could be transported over dirt roads. The Old Leonard Estate was located about twelve miles from the Drayton community. Luella's brother-in-law Paten willingly assumed the responsibility of transporting his children, his brother's children, and many other children to Drayton to Sunday School.

There were four churches in the Drayton Community, two attended by white citizens and two attended by black citizens. All four churches were located on the west side of River Road within three miles of each other. White citizens attended the Drayton Baptist Church and the Drayton Methodist Church. Black and racially mixed citizens attended Macedonia Baptist and Shady Grove Methodist Churches. Shady Grove and Macedonia shared the old Drayton Colored Cemetery located at the rear of Macedonia Baptist Church. According to Macedonia Baptist Church's history, there had not been any integrated church services between Black and White citizens since the 1870s. Prior to the 1870s, Black and White citizens worshipped together according to their church denomination.

Figure 25: Luella's brother-in-Law Paten

CHAPTER 5 ~ World War II, Motherhood and Farm Life - 1940-1949

The years between 1940 and 1949 were stressful ones in Luella's life. First, her oldest child was diagnosed with epilepsy. Shortly thereafter, her father, whom she was very fond of, died. Because both Luella and James believed that children were a gift from God, they were also extremely blessed during that period. God blessed them with their first daughter in September of 1942. Sixteen months later, they were blessed with another son, Elijah. Elijah was named in honor of James' brother who served in the U.S. Army during World War I.

Luella had hoped for another girl to provide Christine a playmate because the Beal family male offspring far out-numbered females. In 1944, James and Luella were the parents of four sons and one daughter. The oldest son by then was a thirteen-year-old. During this period, Luella was very saddened by the death of her husband's sister-in-law, Lillie.

While the country was engaged in World War II overseas, Luella and James were actively making love at home. In 1945, they gave birth to their second daughter, Ruby. They were happy because their first daughter now had a female playmate. This was important because there were no other children on the farm in this age group.

The rapid increase in their household required James and Luella to develop a system of care for younger family members, especially during planting and harvesting seasons. This system of care assigned certain responsibilities to older children. John Frank (JF) was assigned the responsibility and care of Christine, who was fondly referred to as JF's child. Elijah was assigned to James (Happy) and referred to as Happy's child. Ruby was assigned to Marion (Melvin) and became Marion's child.

Exactly fifteen months after Ruby's birth, Luella gave birth to another girl, Mary, their third daughter and seventh child. Mary, by default, became a mama's child. She was named in honor of Luella's mother-in-law and the sister-in-law who first introduced her to James.

Two years and three days after the birth of Mary, Luella and James received another blessing with the birth of their fourth daughter, Beatrice. Beatrice, fondly called Bea by family members, did not have a designation of belonging to anyone and became a "child of the house." Everyone pitched in to care for Bea.

In 1948, Luella's brother-in-law Paten remarried and brought his new bride to the farm. Shortly thereafter, they became guardians for two young girls - Betty (age two) and Dorothy (age three). Betty and Dorothy became an integral part of the Beal extended family.

During the 1930s, one of Paten's first cousins joined the Beal family, and he served as a part-time guardian for all the Beal children on the Old Leonard Estate. His name was Eugene, but nicknames were attached to many individuals, and he was no exception. He was called "Son Collier" by most adults and "Cousin Son" by the children.

Throughout the 1940s, Luella and James entertained a host of family members and friends in their home. There were annual visits from family members who had moved to northern states during the "Great Migration" between 1915 and the 1940s. That period witnessed many agricultural workers leaving farms in the south for factory work in the north. Also, many females traveled north for live-in jobs such as cooks, maids, and nannies.

Two of Luella's brothers migrated to New Jersey and two of James' brothers migrated to New York State. James' youngest sister, Mary Alice migrated to Michigan. Several of Luella's first cousins migrated to all the above states.

Luella's brother Alexander (Alex) who migrated to New Jersey died in 1946. Luella had a close relationship with all her siblings, but she had a special bond with Alex, who wanted to send her to college.

Two of Luella's siblings relocated to Chattanooga, Tennessee during the 1930s and two sisters and one brother relocated to various cities in Florida. Luella received visits and maintained correspondence with many extended family members even while taking care of her large family.

By the late 1940s, on occasions, she would leave her husband and older children in charge and travel by train with the two youngest children to visit her oldest sister in Tallahassee, FL.

Figure 26: Luella's Father-in-law and step-mother-in-law

The Old Leonard Estate was located on the Crisp and Dooly County line. It was physically closer to the Piney Grove Community than to the Drayton Community. Like Drayton, Piney Grove operated a church school for elementary grades. Black children who lived on the Old Leonard Estate and surrounding farms walked to the Piney Grove School. Luella developed close personal relationships with several individuals in the Piney Grove Community and throughout Crisp and Dooly counties during the 1940s.

The rapid growth in her household compelled Luella to obtain female support for the care of her daughters. Luella did not know how to braid or plait hair; therefore, with four girls, she had to solicit help from others in grooming their hair. Two older nieces of Luella's gave her support for short periods of time. However, since they were teenagers and in school, their time was limited. Luella paid Eunice, the wife of a young couple living on an adjacent farm, to groom her daughters' hair. Her relationship with Cousin Son became more dependent because he would frequently visit and assist with the supervision of her younger children during short periods of absence.

Luella's relationship with schoolteachers at the Piney Grove Church School became more regular and intimate during the latter part of the 1940s. Her daughter Christine entered first grade in 1948 and her fourth son Elijah entered first grade the following year. Luella appealed to teachers to allow Elijah to enroll early so that Christine would not have to walk almost two miles to school alone. There were no other children on the Old Leonard Estate Christine's age. There were a few children on the adjacent farm close to Christine's age; however, they took a different route to school.

Luella's mother, Rena, also made periodic long stays with her family. Luella's oldest brother Levi (Buck) and his wife Emma Rose from Atlanta were frequent visitors from out of town. They did not have any children; however, they served as temporary guardians to a host of nieces and nephews. Luella's second oldest sister Julia, her husband and three children, made annual summer visits from Chattanooga. One other frequent visitor from out of town to the Old Leonard Estate was James' cousin Walter Hodo from Detroit.

Figure 27: Luella's Family

CHAPTER 6 ~ Excessive Family Challenges and Losses - 1950-1959

Luella conceived her ninth child, a son, in January of 1950. It is ironic that she experienced the death of her first born child, JF, in March of the same year. It is said that a child is a blessing from God. It is very difficult for most parents to absorb the death of a child, regardless of how old that child may be at the time of death.

The biblical passage that may best describe Luella's acceptance of JF's death is from the book of Revelations, chapter fourteen, verse thirteen, "And I heard a voice from heaven saying unto me, Write, blessed are the dead which die in the Lord from henceforth: Yea, saith the Spirit, that they may rest from their labours; and their works do follow them."

Luella's actions and her attention to her family after JF's funeral were steadfast. The quote by an unknown author that best describes her acceptance of his death is "Love is stronger than death; it can't stop death from happening, but no matter how hard death tries, it can't separate people from love. It cannot take away our memories, either. In the end, life is stronger than death."

Luella kept JF's memory alive by sharing with his younger siblings information about his character. Luella was very proud of her first born. She would tell her younger children that their oldest brother was a very loving and thoughtful person. She often said that he was a very obedient and easy-going child.

Therefore, it is no wonder that the male child born six months after the death of JF appeared to have many of JF's personality traits, although his physical features closely resembled those of Luella's third child Marion. The ninth child, a son, was given the name Jimmy. Jimmy was a very active and easy-going child who rarely cried. However, when his look-a-like brother who enlisted in the United States Army during the Korean Conflict returned home on leave in uniform, it seemed like nothing could control his fears and tears. It took all of Luella's coercing to convince Jimmy that Marion was not a stranger but his older brother in uniform. Luella was quick to recognize that Marion's long absence in the mind of her toddler had caused Jimmy to forget Marion's facial image. She realized that because the only picture hanging over the fireplace was a picture of JF, her toddler may have thought that his oldest brother had come back from the dead in uniform.

After Marion had remained home for several days, he and Jimmy became reacquainted and developed a strong brotherly bond. This made

Luella very happy. Luella and James received support and assistance from his siblings, his father, and his stepmother. James' oldest sister, Eva and her husband Dan invited their third daughter, Mary to live with them on the Evans' Estate located near Macedonia Baptist Church in Drayton. Dan was an entertaining visitor because he usually brought his Jew Harp and entertained the family. When a house became vacant on the Old Leonard Estate, Dan and Eva moved to be closer to her family in their senior years. Since, they were now located only across the field from James and Luella, Mary returned home to live with the rest of her siblings. Two days prior to her husband's 52nd birthday and two years after the birth of her fifth son, Luella gave birth to her tenth child, a fifth daughter. Luella named her fifth daughter in honor of her childhood playmate and oldest niece Vesta.

She informed her husband that she was finished having children; to underscore her decision, she gave her tenth child the nickname "Babychild." It is not certain if she made that decision independently or only because her last child was allergic to both mother's milk and cows' milk. Luella's husband had to drive almost forty miles one way to purchase goat's milk for their last-born child. The expense was not an issue; however, timing was an issue because the last child was born during harvest season for cotton and peanuts.

Another important factor that may have influenced Luella's decision to not have any more babies was the brain surgery that her oldest daughter Christine underwent to remove a tumor from her brain. The brain surgery affected Christine's optic nerve and she became legally blind. Surgeons and physicians at the Talmadge Memorial Hospital in Augusta, Georgia advised Luella to enroll Christine in the Academy for the Blind in Macon, Georgia after her recovery from the initial surgery. Since Christine was only ten years old, Luella wanted her to continue her education. Therefore, in the fall of 1953, Christine moved into a dormitory at the Academy for the Blind and continued her education. Earlier that year Luella's son Happy married Patience Tolbert.

"Family practice is extremely rewarding. You are involved with families from birth through their grandparent years. You become involved with people's lives and understand the trials and tribulations that every family faces." The previous quote by James Kramer symbolizes Luella's life purpose. She became a grandmother eighteen months after the birth of her last child. Unfortunately, six months later, her first grandchild, Joseph, died due to acute diarrhea. His death disheartened Luella, and she was overheard telling her daughter-in-law, "Had you brought this child to me earlier, I could have saved him."

Luella's inquisitive daughter Mary asked, "What did you mean about being able to save Joseph?"

In Luella's typical fashion, she conducted a bit of hands-on teaching. She said to Mary, "Come outside to the flower garden with me." Standing near the flower garden in the front yard, Luella pointed to a viny flower with purple blooms and said, "If you boil the blooms from this plant and mix it with baby's milk, it will cure diarrhea in a short period of time. Diarrhea causes dehydration and dehydration causes death."

It seemed that Luella's immediate family would continue to endure various challenges during the 1950s. Two months prior to the death of Joseph, Luella and James' house was destroyed in a fire. It was largely because of James' asthmatic condition that the family received no injuries because of the fire. The fire occurred in the pre-dawn hours on Mother's Day. The fire ignited because a window fell on an electrical extension cord that was used to keep baby chicks warm in a brooder on the outside of the house. All the family's personal belongings were lost except for the contents of the guest bedroom. Due to the compassion of extended family members and neighbors, Luella's large family did not become homeless. There were three other houses on the Old Leonard Estate and family members were dispersed throughout those homes for a few days. With all the confusion caused by the fire, no one recalls whether the baby chicks survived the fire.

Luella's brother-in-law and father-in-law initiated a search for another house. Another house comparable to the one that burned down was located on another property owned by the Leonard Estate. The new house was moved to the exact spot where the burned down house had stood. Neither the smoke house nor the barn was damaged by the fire.

It took several weeks to make the new house move-in ready. Fortunately, a White neighbor to the east of James and Luella allowed them to use an empty house on his farm while their new house was being prepared for occupancy.

During the fall of 1954, Happy was hit in the head by a fellow worker. A messenger appeared at James and Luella's house and informed them that their son had received a head wound. Although it was late at night when the messenger arrived, Luella and James asked nearby family members to check on their younger children because they had to travel almost seventy miles to see about their child, Happy. When it came to Luella's children, if she could move mountains to ensure their well-being, she would readily have done so.

That same year the United States Supreme Court declared in its landmark decision, Brown v. Board of Education of Topeka, that state laws establishing separate public schools for Black and White students denied Black children's equal educational opportunities. That decision had far-reaching effects in rural southern communities.

As late as 1956, many children in rural communities were attending school in church facilities, while independent schools had been built and were operated with taxpayer dollars for White students. In some cases, the local Board of Education provided certified teachers to teach in church school settings.

When speculation began about the closing of church schools, Luella began planning for her children to continue their elementary school education. She allowed Elijah to live with her brother-in-law Frank in Brooklyn, New York and her daughter Ruby to live with an educator, Mrs. Clara, and Mr. Scott in Cordele. By that time, her second oldest son, Happy had married and started his own family. Elijah did not remain in Brooklyn for an extended period, largely because his uncle lived in a mixed neighborhood and his father expressed concerns about Elijah's ability to readjust to segregated life in South Georgia.

Luella did not share all her husband's views; however, she presented a united front in the presence of their children. Luella said to her husband, "One will never know what he or she is able to do unless he first tries and tries and tries again." James became more concerned during a visit by his brother when Elijah's best friend was described as a young white girl named Maria. After the publicizing of the death of Emmett Till for looking and speaking to a white woman, James was adamant about bringing his child back to Georgia.

Luella welcomed Elijah home – and welcomed the extra pair of hands to perform chores on the farm. It should be noted that James and Luella shared an amicable and cooperative relationship with their White neighbors.

Luella's daughter, Mary, recalled one tense event that occurred in the 1950s involving the wife of a White tenant on a neighboring farm. On a cold winter night in 1955, there was a knock at the door. Usually, when there was a knock late at night, it signified some sort of distress. Luella answered the door and saw the lady whom she recognized as the wife of the sharecropper on the Bolden's Farm standing in the cold, barefoot and wearing a torn negligee. Luella, having seen that the lady was bruised and bloody, assessed the situation as a domestic violence incident. Luella said to the lady, "Here is a pair of house shoes and a bath robe, put them on and keep running." Later, Luella's daughter Mary asked, "Mama, why did you tell her to keep on running?" Luella answered her daughter, "Child, your daddy is away and there is nothing to stop that angry man from coming here and hurting us. If someone is that mad to beat his wife like that, there is no telling what he will do to someone that helps her."

CHAPTER 7 ~ Transition to City Life and Rock & Roll Music – 1950-1959

Farm life, especially the planting and harvesting of crops, had become arduous for James and Luella since all the young men had left the farm. James' asthmatic condition grew worse. Therefore, in the fall of 1956, they agreed it was time to leave the farm and move into town.

Luella's husband, James, selected a house on a busy road; however, she did not like it because of the imminent danger for her children. They moved to the Newtown neighborhood south of Cordele. Instead of her small children riding a school bus for ten miles one way, they would be able to walk to school. One other factor that may have influenced the family move into Cordele was the birth of their first granddaughter who lived in Cordele.

The move into town brought new challenges for the family. Although the house into which the family moved had more modern amenities than the house on the farm, it was much smaller, and the yard was much smaller. The new house did not have pecan or fruit trees. However, Luella never encountered any difficulty in making new friends, and her children profited from her gregarious spirit.

The Perry family had recently moved to Newtown, and they had five children whose ages basically aligned with five children in the Beal family. Hence, the children adjusted quickly to their new environment.

The family member who did not adjust very well to the family move was Luella's husband. He was 56 years old and most of his work experience was farming. He worked for a while as a freelance carpenter; however, he did not generate sufficient income to take care of his large family. Luella and James discussed the situation with their two oldest sons, and it was agreed that James would go to Florida and live with their son Marion, to look for employment there. Luella was comfortable with this decision because she had a sister and a brother who resided in that same county in Florida.

During the fourteenth month of James' employment in Florida, fate would present a tragedy and another challenge to the Beal family. On Tuesday, February 18, five days after Luella's 48th birthday, her son Elijah was accidentally killed by a shotgun blast to his head. A reprint of the article that appeared in the local newspaper, The Cordele Dispatch, February 19, 1958:

The article did not share information that Elijah was accidentally killed with his paternal grandfather's shotgun. Nor did the article mention that Elijah should have been in school at the time of the shooting. He was not in school because he was serving a three-day out of school suspension for shooting a rubber band in class.

Elijah's father returned home for his funeral and remained there permanently. James carried a sense of guilt because he was not at home when that accident occurred. He deeply regretted that his wife Luella had to face alone the immediate impact of Elijah's death and the added burden of consoling the younger children.

More importantly, many people do not know that Luella was basically, the first respondent to this accident. The oldest youth who was the

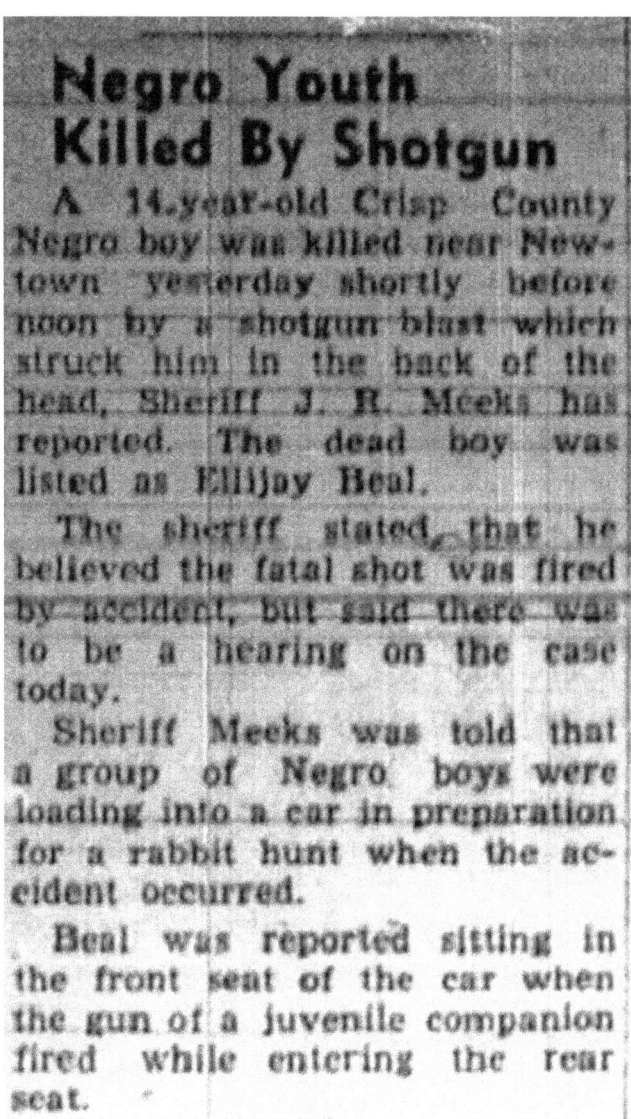

Figure 28: Newspaper Clipping from 1958

driver of the vehicle did not know anything to do but take Elijah to his mother. Therefore, she saw a child to whom she had given birth with his brains blown out through the front of his head. It is through the Grace of God that she was able to withstand this tragedy and keep her family on solid ground.

The family's financial situation became difficult because of James' decision to return home permanently without a job or a steady source of income. Luella decided to look for work outside the home. She readily found work with the Bush family who owned a corner store. She prepared two meals a day for the Bush family and occasionally assisted them in their store.

Luella taught her children how to take care of each other. Luella and her children performed farm work by joining work crews and traveling to various farms on a truck owned by Mr. Arthur Cobb. All money earned by the children was used to assist with household expenses, except what they earned on Saturdays.

Luella and James welcomed their second granddaughter and third grandchild in 1959. Luella and James decided to move to a larger house that was less expensive than the house in which they were staying. However, the new house did not have the amenities of the first house. The new location was also in the Newtown area but in the older section. Both Luella and her children gained additional friends because of that move.

It was around this time that Luella demonstrated the wisdom of Solomon and administered tough love by way of memorable non-physical punishments to her children. Her daughter Ruby recalled the following event about her mother, Luella. "I must tell a story to give her memorial comment. I was about 11 or 12 years old, and Mom had all the children working and cleaning all day. We washed the clothes, hung them up on the line, took clothes in, and performed detailed spring cleaning."

"At the end of this day, Mom and Mary cooked dinner. I am an avid reader, and I never liked to cook, so I read the Bible while Mom and Mary cooked dinner. Once dinner had been prepared and we sat down at the dinner table, she told me 'Ruby you may go read the Bible!" Ruby did not eat dinner that day. Also, for the record, she still does not like to cook; however, she can prepare a meal if it is necessary. Shortly after the incident with Ruby, Luella's daughter Mary received a dose of her wisdom for not paying attention to an assigned task. Mary was baking biscuits and went outside to play, and the bread burned. Luella told Mary, "You will eat every one of those burnt biscuits. The pan contained twelve burnt biscuits. Mary learned a lesson and became the family's baker for years.

Luella gave birth to two children during the 1950s. Her daughter-in-law, Patience gave birth to four children during the same decade. Two of Luella's children and one grandchild died during that decade. Rapid changes occurred in the society that threatened to have a significant impact on family values. However, James and Luella presented a united front when it came to raising children, academic expectations, obedience, self-respect, and respect for others - and especially respect for elderly persons. Those expectations applied to their children and grandchildren and children of neighbors and close acquaintances.

Although it was widely known throughout the family that Luella was the primary disciplinarian, she was strongly supported and backed by her husband. When one of their children would seek James' permission to visit neighbors or attend an event, including church, he usually responded "Did you ask your mother and what did she say?"

James had unyielding confidence in Luella's sound judgment and fairness. They had shared almost thirty years of marriage, and he had witnessed her resourcefulness, compassion, and industrious nature. He knew that she was an excellent mother and a faithful partner.

On the night, several years earlier, when their house burned down, he witnessed her return into the burning structure just to get the portrait of her oldest child hanging above a mantel piece. He breathed a sigh of relief when she appeared on the bottom doorstep just as the roof fell in. He had also learned that it was wise to consult with her on issues affecting the family.

Undoubtedly, he recalled the only time that Luella became highly upset with him and displayed her displeasure in front of their children. Several years prior to their move from the farm, James sold a bull calf without consulting Luella, and she verbally enunciated her dissatisfaction.

They refrained from purchasing a television set for many years. However, to keep their children from presenting creative excuses to visit the home of a neighbor, who did have a television set, Luella acquiesced and bought a television set. Luella's children believed she bought the television set to keep them at home under her eagle-like watchful eyes. Luella displayed her intelligence and her forward thinking by purchasing a television set with a detachable cord. She would detach the cord and not re-attach it until all school homework and household chores had been performed.

Teenagers were drawn to the television show "American Bandstand" with Dick Clark in the late 1950s. Although Luella's children had been exposed to Rhythm and Blues on the radio, live dancing and music on the television were not perceived by James and Luella as something that provided positive development. In the 1950s with a rockin' piano, Fats Domino outsold every fifty rock and roll pioneer except Elvis Presley. James and Luella were concerned about their three teenage girls listening to such lyrics as "I Found My Thrill on Blueberry Hill." They wanted their children to succeed in life, and they did not want them looking for a "thrill on Blueberry Hill." Luella encouraged all her children to grow spiritually. During their early childhood days, Luella taught all her children the Lord's Prayer and insisted that they memorize it and repeat it nightly before retiring for bed. She and James reinforced the spiritual training for their children by requiring each child to say a Bible verse after the food was blessed at each meal. No one could take a serving of food until this routine had been completed. Everyone had to be seated at the table before the food was blessed. Therefore, giving thanks and praying were ingrained parts of life in the Beal household.

Both Luella and James were deeply spiritual individuals. They were not religious fanatics and allowed their children a certain amount of latitude. When their children indicated they wanted to be saved by God and be baptized, Luella and James supported their choices. Two of Luella's children were sprinkled in the Shady Grove Methodist Church. Most individuals received their identity from others, from the expectations of friends and colleagues, from the labels society puts on them, and from the influence of family. Those two children were highly influenced by their uncle who was a steward in the Shady Grove Methodist Church. They were later baptized in the neighboring Baptist church. Luella and James did not express any concerns about their choice. They simply wanted their children to live Christian lives. They truly believed that if one were a Christian, he or she would no longer allow others to tell them who they were. Both Luella and James thought that if one became a Christian one received instructions from God and their actions would adhere to Christ-like principles.

James and Luella therefore had confidence in their children and relied upon the training they had provided them. Luella often quoted Biblical passages to her children. Another one of her favorite verses was Proverbs 22:1, "A good name is rather to be chosen than great riches, and loving favour rather than silver and gold."

Luella's children sometimes believed she knew the entire book of Proverbs verbatim. She often quoted, "Train up a child the way he should go and when he is old, he will not depart from it." Her children were permitted to participate in social and extra–curricular events that were conducted at school, community facilities and churches. If they participated or attended events out of town, they had to be accompanied by an older chaperone. Luella often relayed to her children that she raised them the way her parents raised her.

She would often quote her father by saying, "Show me the company you keep, and I will tell you who you are." She sometimes added, "Birds of a feather flock together." Luella was a strong believer in, "Spare the rod, and spoil the child." She rarely spared the rod.

After Elijah's death, Luella's trust in the public high school administration's commitment to work with parents on disciplinary matters was almost non-existent. She strongly felt that Elijah should have been in school as opposed to going on a rabbit hunt the day he was accidentally killed. She was overheard saying prior to Elijah's death, "The teacher should have contacted me before unilaterally suspending Elijah without a parent conference."

Therefore, she decided that her younger children would attend the private Christian high school, Holsey-Cobb Institute. Her three oldest children attended the private high school, Gillespie-Selden Institute. However, Gillespie-Selden closed when the new Black high school, A. S. Clark, was built and opened in 1956.

Since Luella had established close friendships with many educators in Crisp County, she would often seek their advice. The first house the family lived in when they moved to town was owned by a former principal of Holsey-Cobb Institute, Reverend Lucious Pitts. That house was located across the street from the principal of Southview Elementary School, Mr. George Tutt. Therefore, Luella became very good friends with the Tutt family. She often sought Mr. Tutt's advice on matters pertaining to the education of her younger children. In addition, Mrs. Mary Lewis, a friend, and fellow church member, was also a teacher living in the neighborhood. As a matter of fact, the house that Luella had built in 1970 is located next door to Mrs. Lewis' former house.

A young couple lived on the next corner and were both schoolteachers. The husband taught high school in adjacent Dooly

County and the wife taught elementary school in Crisp County. Luella maintained a close relationship with this couple for more than 50 years. Her daughters performed babysitting services for this couple and her grandchildren became classmates and playmates with the Roberson's children.

Luella had a special way of obtaining information from people. She would customarily ask her children's friends and visitors this question, "Who are your folks?" That question sometimes appeared to momentarily embarrass three of her children who completed elementary school during the fifties and continued to high school. Luella wanted to have firsthand knowledge about her children's friends. Therefore, she developed a special relationship with her children's friends' parents.

Luella was an effective organizer and a very civic-minded individual. She served as catalyst on family, community, and church initiatives. She was very influential because she knew so many people from all walks of life. She appeared to have had a seamless interface with all of them.

Luella entertained professional individuals as well as farm workers as though they were just as important as her family members. She unofficially adopted many of them into her large extended family. Whenever she adopted an individual into the family, she expanded her realm of influence at least tenfold.

Luella was the key individual who initiated the "Busy Bee Christmas Savings Club." This was clearly an example of economic empowerment. The purpose of the club was to set aside money weekly or monthly for the exclusive purpose of having financial resources available during the Christmas holiday season.

Once funds were placed on deposit in the club, they could not be withdrawn until the time specified in the club's by-laws which was the latter part of the month of November. She was a charter member and held basically every office in the club.

She continued her membership in the Macedonia Baptist Church and its missionary society as president. She was a very active member in the Parent Teacher Association throughout her children and grandchildren's enrollment in elementary and secondary school. The decade of the 1950s ended with all of Luella's children enrolled in school.

As a long-time member of the Macedonia Baptist Church – Drayton, Luella earned the respect and admiration of many individuals who frequently attended church services there. When Macedonia Church officers veered from traditions and brought personal politics into the church, Luella would verbalize her displeasure.

Because of her no-nonsense approach even in church affairs, she probably was not bestowed the title "Mother of the Church" that had been traditionally given to the oldest living active female member. She may have been slightly disappointed when a younger female was bestowed the title, but she continued to support the church and give thanks to God.

She served as president of the missionary society and attended church conferences and church association meetings for many years. Prior to the church adding the kitchen annex, she cooked and prepared food during every event when the church served meals. Even after the completion of the kitchen annex, Luella would supply the church with her homemade cream cheese pound cakes.

CHAPTER 8 ~ Civil Rights Era, College, Voting Rights - 1960-1969

Luella encountered many challenges and triumphs during the decade of the 1960s. Her children believed she was born with a drive and determination that could move mountains. They were constantly amazed by her strength of character and her resoluteness concerning almost every challenge she faced, including their education.

Luella's youngest son, Jimmy once stated, "My mother has a direct pipeline to God Almighty."

A challenge that first surfaced for Luella in the 1950s resurfaced in the 1960s. The growth of a brain tumor in her oldest daughter Christine required many return trips to the Talmadge Memorial Hospital in Augusta, Georgia for a second brain surgery and follow-up examinations.

Luella was determined to be physically present in the hospital room at Christine's bedside when she woke up from surgery. The second surgery left Christine totally blind. After the second brain surgery, the medical staff recommended that Christine remain at home and not return to the Academy for the Blind in Macon. The medical staff said the brain tissue would continue to grow and that Christine should have close supervision probably for the rest of her life.

Luella never neglected any of her children; she seemed to be there whenever anyone needed her assistance. She also helped other family members, friends, church members and neighbors. During the fall of 1960, her mother, Surena became ill. Luella's mother resided with her youngest sister Brooksie about ten miles away in the town of Arabi. Luella did not drive; she therefore used her ingenuity and her people skills and arranged with the school bus driver to allow her to travel to Arabi on the school bus in the evening and return to town when he brought students to school the next morning. Luella maintained this routine for almost two months.

She was in the room with her mother when she took her last breath. However, Luella had taken a nap and her oldest brother, Buck, who was also by his mother's side, touched Luella on the shoulder and said "Bunch, mama is gone."

Because Surena was the oldest daughter of Abe and Julia Massey, the Fields, Massey, and Campbell clans came from many parts of the United States to bid their final farewell to Surena. There were five generations present at Surena's funeral. Surena and John's children were a close-knit family unit. Her sons often came to visit their mom and to provide financial support to their sisters, especially their oldest brother, Buck.

Surena died at the age of 90. At the time of her death, she had four sisters, five daughters and five sons living. She was buried at Traveler's Rest Cemetery in Macon County, Georgia. That was the first time many family members had visited the historical burial site of many of the Fields family ancestors.

It was at that funeral that various family members made a pack to keep in touch and organize a family reunion to celebrate happy times and not just meet at funerals.

Christine continued to improve; therefore, Luella found work outside the home. The family needed additional income because Luella decided her younger children would continue to attend the private high school in town. She accepted a job working the 3:00 p.m. - 11:00 p.m. shift as a short order cook for a local motel. The tips she received supplemented her income. During that time, James was home with the children and attended parent-teacher meetings.

Luella was a strict disciplinarian but prided herself in not spanking a child when she was angry. She also said to her children, "I will not leave a scar on you, but I will put something on you that soap and water will not wash off." Luella had the memory of an elephant; and when she began to spank a child, she would cite a list of infractions done since the last spanking.

Luella's spankings were mild compared to her lectures. Many times, her children would rather have gotten spankings than her lectures. They also preferred a spanking to her pinching. She pinched like her mother did. Both she and her mother would grab the inside of the upper arm where it was very tender and twist the skin until the recipient thought that skin itself would peel off. Her spankings left them sore for a short period of time, but the words in her lectures lasted for decades.

Luella's children often thought she missed her calling in life. They truly believed she would have been an excellent child psychologist or psychiatrist. Different ones of her children tested her patience; however, Luella would almost always demonstrate her quick wit and high level of intelligence. She added new ways to punish misbehaving children other than by physical means.

Luella would take away privileges when they seemed to be most cherished. An example is when her daughter, Mary, brought a college classmate home. They both went out on dates and missed getting home by the established curfew.

Luella did not say one word when they arrived home long past midnight. However, the next morning, both Mary and her college classmate were awakened at dawn and told that they had work to do. Luella added her usual refrain, "If you are woman enough to stay out all night, you are woman enough to work all day."

There were several incidents that involved Luella's daughter Bea. Bea would tarry in doing homework and household chores. She also had a serious sweet tooth. Therefore, it appeared that Bea gave Luella an opportunity to become more creative with various forms of discipline. Luella would exercise patience during the week, then deliver her disciplinary punishment on a beautiful Sunday afternoon. Just when it was the usual time for children to go outside and play with friends or visit others in the neighborhood, Luella would instruct Bea to go to bed and only get up to use the bathroom. Other times, Luella would not allow her children to attend the annual county fair knowing they had eagerly anticipated its arrival.

There were several types of infractions that would prompt Luella to administer immediate disciplinary action while others did not appear as pressing. All of Luella's children and grandchildren soon learned that one did not perform any act that could be conceived as lying, stealing, or cheating.

These acts caused Luella to administer disciplinary action closely related to the death sentence. Probably the second most severe punishment was delivered for a child sassing a parent or another older person.

The third category of unacceptable acts and behaviors by Luella's children and grandchildren that caused her to mete out various forms of disciplinary actions was fighting. Luella truly believed in loving one another and in no way was fighting in that formula. Not performing assigned chores was important, but punishment for those infractions just did not add up to those acts and behaviors that helped build one's character. Administration of disciplinary acts by Luella was not reserved only for her children and grandchildren. It applied to any child under her supervision or in her presence who performed an unacceptable act or behavior.

The year following the death of her mother, Surena, Luella's Aunt Rosabelle died in Valdosta, Georgia. Aunt Rosabelle was the primary caregiver for Luella's youngest aunt, Eva, who had spent 25 years in a mental health facility. The question now was who will take care of Aunt Eva since Aunt Rosabelle has died? Eva did not have any children of her own.

Luella stepped up to the plate and assumed that responsibility in 1961. Because everyone present after the funeral was looking from one to the other, Luella spoke to her third oldest son, Marion, and said, "Put her in your car. I am taking her home with me." That was the end of that discussion.

Holsey Cobb Institute, the Black private high school, closed in 1962. A decision was made to send Luella's three high school students to the Black public high school. This was because the family could not afford tuition and room and board at a private school outside the commuting distance. School integration had not taken place in Cordele during 1962; therefore, because of financial reasons, Luella had no choice but to send her children to the public Black school, A. S. Clark. However, she felt confident in sending her children to A. S. Clark since her former neighbor and friend, George Tutt was appointed the new principal.

This school was built after the 1954 Supreme Court Decision, Brown vs. the Topeka, Kansas Board of Education. A. S. Clark opened in 1956 as a public school for Blacks for grades 1 thru 12.

During the fall of 1962, Luella's third oldest sister, Eula's oldest son, Howard, died in South Florida. Howard was one of Luella's favorite nephews. It probably was because he had a marvelous sense of humor and Luella enjoyed a good sense of humor. Luella's purpose in life appeared to be to support family in times of need and during the loss of a loved one. Her brother, Buck, drove from Atlanta and picked up Luella and her youngest sister in Cordele and drove them to South Florida to attend Howard's funeral.

The next year Luella was delighted that her second oldest daughter Ruby graduated with honors from the first and only public Black high school in Cordele. This was a triumph for Luella because she dreamed of the day when one of her children would continue their education and go on to college.

However, this triumph was very short lived because two mornings after Ruby's high school graduation, Luella's husband of 33 years succumbed to a bronchial heart attack. Therefore, the family had to curtail their graduation celebration and plan a funeral. It was even more challenging because the day after her husband's death, her daughter Ruby reached her 18th birthday. Somehow, Luella, with the aid of her brother-in-law, Paten, and her youngest sister, was able to plan the funeral and console six young children at the same time.

Her husband's death left Luella with the sole responsibility of raising six children and caring for an aunt. One of these children had a physical handicap – blindness. The children often heard their mom singing the old hymn, "*The Lord Will Make a Way Somehow*" by Thomas A. Dorsey.

Figure 29: "The Lord Will Make a Way Somehow" by Thomas A. Dorsey.

Like a ship that is tossed and driven, Battered by an angry sea,
When the storms of life are raging And their fury falls on me,
I wonder what I have done That makes this race so hard to run,
Then I say to my soul, take courage, The Lord will make a way some-how.
Try to do my best in service, Try to live the best I can,
When I choose to do the right thing, Evil's present on every hand
I look up and wonder why That good fortune pass me by
Then I say to my soul, be patient, The Lord will make a way some-how.
Often there is misunderstanding Out of all the good I do,
Go to friends for consolation And I find them complaining too,
So many nights I toss in pain, Wondering what the day will bring,
But I say to my heart do not worry, The Lord will make a way some-how.
`Often times she recited her mantra, the twenty third Psalms:
The Lord is my shepherd; I shall not want.
He maketh me to lie down in green pastures:
He leadeth me beside the still waters
He restoreth my soul; he leadeth me in the
Path of righteousness for his name's sake.
Yea, though I walk through the valley of the
Shadow of death, I will fear no evil: for thou
Art with me; thy rod and thy staff they comfort me.
Thou preparest a table before me in the presence of
Enemies: thou anointest my head with oil; my cup runneth over.
Surely goodness and mercy shall follow me all the
Days of my life; and I shall dwell in the house of the
Lord forever.

With six children between the ages 11 and 21, at the age of 53, Luella needed all the inspiration and help she could get. Partially because her husband died only two days after her first child graduated from high school and Mama had plans for her to attend college. Mama received the support and encouragement from her long-time friend and educator, Mrs. Janet Pace, the daughter of Mrs. Clara Scott, and she turned to her Aunt Vic and her first cousin Rosa in Savannah for assistance.

Luella appealed to them on behalf of Ruby for room and board so that Ruby could enroll at Savannah State College in the fall of 1963. In the meantime, Luella, and several of her children, including college bound Ruby, were picking cotton when Dr. Martin Luther King, Jr. delivered his "I Have Dream" speech during the March on Washington in the summer of 1963. Luella's first cousin and aunt agreed, and Ruby became a freshman that fall semester.

Luella was fulfilling one of her dreams when she took Ruby to Savannah a week later to enroll at Savannah State College. Luella decided what college Ruby would attend. She respected the advice of teachers and principals when they advised her that her children should go to college or trade school.

Happy and Marion served as Luella's chauffeurs for many years. Since Happy lived nearby, he drove Luella to many out-of-town locations for various purposes. During the birth of Happy's seventh child, he was driving Luella and Ruby back to Savannah after her first Christmas break. It was a memorable and frightful day because Cordele experienced a severe ice storm the night prior to their departure. There were no interstate highways at that time and travel occurred mostly on two-lane roads.

The spring of the following year, Luella's youngest sister, Brooksie and her husband decided to move their family to upstate New York to join several of their older children. Luella's brother-in-law, Henry, had gotten too old to make a living from farming. That was a mild blow to Luella because she and her youngest sister had never lived more than twenty-five miles away from each other their entire lives until then. They had shared so many visits, meals, and conversations and those were sorely missed.

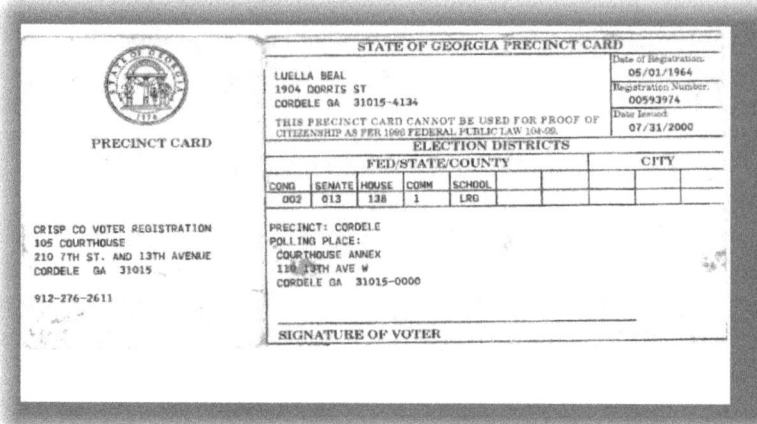

Figure 29a: Luella's Voter Registration

Luella was not devastated about her sister's move because she was elated that her third daughter, Mary, also graduated with honors from A. S. Clark High School. She began making plans for Mary to join Ruby and enroll in Savannah State College in the Fall.

Mary did not want to go to college because she wanted to find a job to help lessen the financial burden the family faced. Luella adamantly refused to entertain my argument and reaffirmed her position that Mary would attend college in the fall. Luella received small amounts of financial assistance and support from her son Marion; her brother-in-law, Paten; her brothers and other relatives and close friends.

Luella did, not only train her children in domestic science, but instilled in them the importance of helping their family survive. When her youngest son, Jimmy was old enough to work, he obtained a job at the local Holiday Inn. He contributed funds to help the family get their first telephone.

By 1966, Luella's daughter-in-law, Patience had given birth to five more children. This brought Luella's total number of grandchildren to eight. During the Christmas holidays of 1966, her grandson, Nathaniel, who was born in 1962, asked his grandmother, Luella, if he could live with her all the time. Luella agreed because Ruby and Mary were away at college and Beatrice who graduated from high school was away at trade school, so there was ample space available in the Beal household.

The year 1967 brought more grief to Luella because early that year one of her older sisters, Eula, died unexpectedly in South Florida. Since this was the first death of a close family member since the death of her husband and the departure of Ruby and Mary to college, Luella faced a dilemma. That dilemma was short lived because Luella learned that Mary and Ruby would be on spring break and could come home to care for Christine, their younger siblings, and Aunt Eva.

During the Civil Rights Era, Luella had often stated that it was okay that people were marching to protect our rights; however, she was working to survive and keep her family alive and well. During the month of May 1968, Luella's father-in-law, the patriarch of the Beal clan died around the age of one hundred and two years. Luella's step-mother-in-law, Magnolia, was only three years her senior. Their relationship appeared to strengthen after the death of Luella's father-in-law.

The very next month, Luella's 9th grandchild, a male was born. He was named in honor of Robert Kennedy and his fraternal grandfather. Robert was his fraternal grandfather's middle name and Robert Kennedy was assassinated a few hours before his birth. It was also the date that Luella's husband died five years earlier.

Luella respected the Kennedys because they were brave enough to speak out against injustices in America not just in the South. She had seen an increase in hope for America prior to the assassination of Dr. King and Senator Robert Kennedy. Afterwards, she felt those two assassinations would set America's progress backward for some time.

Ongoing televised demonstrations against the war in Vietnam also lowered her confidence in America's desire or ability to place social and racial injustice at the top of its political agenda. For many years, photos of Dr. King, John and Robert Kennedy hung on the wall in her home.

In August of that year, her daughter Mary graduated from Savannah State College with a degree in accounting. Immediately after attending Mary's college graduation ceremony, Luella, Marion, and Mary left Savannah and drove to Talmadge Memorial Hospital in Augusta to check on Christine. After collaborating with the medical staff and learning that Christine's condition had not improved, Luella decided to remain at the hospital for a few days since Mary would be at home to take care of the household. She also knew from Mary's early life that she would possibly travel, to faraway places.

Mary had informed her mother, when she graduated from high school, that she wanted to join the Peace Corps and visit Latin American countries. Luella intellectually knew it was unlikely that Mary would find employment in Cordele in her chosen career field. Therefore, when Mary announced she was leaving for Syracuse in upstate New York a week or so later, Luella was not surprised.

Christine's condition improved slightly, and she went home to Cordele. However, Christine was home for less than two weeks before she died on Mary's birthday that year.

Bea, who earned a certificate in nursing from Monroe Area Vocational School in Albany that year, moved to Atlanta to reside with Luella's brother Buck and his wife. Jimmy decided shortly after his eighteenth birthday to enlist in the United States Marine Corps and that decision caused a lot of apprehension in the family.

Jimmy did not intend to spend his life working as a dishwasher at the local Holiday Inn, and he knew he either had to work or go to school or both. Therefore, he opted for the Marines to avoid being drafted by the Army. He also saw it as a means for helping the family financially. Luella's apprehensiveness was largely due to negative televised reports on offensives in the war zone.

Jimmy made the following comments many years later. "The impact that mother had on my career choice was that I needed to change it. At 18 years old, I felt I needed to be able to help the family out more. So, I joined the Marine Corps in a time of war. That was the first time I knew I did something to make her cry. 'THAT HURT ME'!

"So, I made it a point to carry myself in a way that would not have that kind of effect on her ever again. I tell the younger generation to trust in God. Love thy neighbor, respect each other."

Bea's move to Jersey City, New Jersey was inspired by Luella and her youngest brother's widow, Sylvia, in 1969. Doc and Sylvia did not have any children.

Luella was not a selfish mother and often shared her children with childless family members. She made many sacrifices to enable her children and grandchildren to have a successful life. Luella did not only teach them about God, but she also taught them about mankind specifically and in general. She would not even entertain the idea of remarrying. Mary specifically recalled Luella saying, "I will not bring another man into this house around my girls."

Figure 30: Luella's home was built in 1970. Several modifications occurred over the 40 years of her occupancy.

Figure 31: Great-grandchildren Ilene, Jerry, Emmanuel, & Christopher

CHAPTER 9 ~ Empty Nest – Not for Long – 1970-1979

There were a lot of major changes in the United States during the 1970s. Until then, little had been done in the South to integrate public schools. States that continued to operate segregated school systems ran the risk of losing federal funds in support of education. Public school integration in Crisp County, Georgia did not have any significant impact on Luella's children because her last born, Vesta graduated from high school in May 1970.

When the Beal family first moved to the Newtown neighborhood, Luella became very close friends with her neighbors, George and Helen Tutt. George was the principal of A. S. Clark High School for almost ten years, and Luella did not hesitate to send her children to A. S. Clark because Mr. Tutt became the principal the same year Holsey Cobb Institute closed.

Luella performed different roles in her relationship with George and Helen. On occasion she would serve as their unofficial spiritual advisor, a sounding board, and she acted as a surrogate grandmother to their children. Luella served as the Tutt family's baker because Helen did not bake.

George could always count on Luella's support at Parent-Teacher Association meetings. Luella was one of his most dedicated parents who did not shy away from parental responsibilities. George had been sought after by several historically Black colleges and universities; therefore, he took advantage of a job offer at Miles College in Birmingham, Alabama. The move did not end their friendship; however, it did reduce the frequency of their interaction.

The decade of the 1960s ended with Luella leading the initiative to construct a house for her family. The family had rented three different houses since moving to the suburbs from the farm. Luella, the industrious and forward-thinking person, appealed to a nephew of her husband years earlier to purchase a lot and hold it for her until she was ready to build. The lot had been previously owned by Luella's youngest sister.

Luella's determination at age fifty-nine amazed construction workers because they witnessed her daily visits to the construction site. She was not a spectator, but actively participated in whatever task she was able to perform to help construct a home of her own. There were many tasks that she accomplished to construct the family's first new house. Its construction was accomplished with the help of immediate and extended family members and friends. Her home construction accomplishment predates

President Jimmy Carter's Habitat for Humanity housing initiatives.

The fall of 1970 presented Luella with an almost empty nest when Vesta departed for college at Savannah State College. However, one grandson decided he wanted to stay with his grandma Luella, moved in and did not leave until after he completed trade school.

Luella's Aunt Eva continued to reside with her until her death in 1980. Luella, the proverbial caregiver, provided care for her older brother, Richard, who was a widower and childless. Furthermore, she also provided periodic refuge for her older brother, John who had a turbulent marriage.

Luella seemed to get that boost of spirit from the Lord to lift her up when she needed it. During the late fall of 1970, her youngest son returned home without any physical wounds from the Vietnam War. He decided not to reside in Cordele, but moved to Rochester, New York with Luella's youngest sister. With four children and a sister in upstate New York, Luella decided to begin traveling on happy occasions.

She would spend several weeks in Upstate New York during the summer months. She alternated between Syracuse and Rochester and would make short visits to her in-laws in Brooklyn.

Figure 32: Luella (right) with youngest sister, and cousin, James Fields in Rochester, NY

There were many happy times and sad times, but through it all, Luella championed family unity. Everywhere she lived, she always found space in her yard for a vegetable garden. When she was away taking care of a family member or attending a funeral in another state, her neighbor Frank Walker would monitor Luella's house and assist with minor chores.

Frank was the equivalent of Vesta's godfather. Frank had been a widower for almost fifteen years and Luella with her kind heart and benevolent manners ensured that Frank was well fed. He had been left partially paralyzed from an automobile accident in the mid-1950s, but Frank did not let his infirmities make him a bitter person. He was always upbeat, and it seems that Luella inspired him and lifted his spirits. He truly loved her soups. He would often tease her that since her maiden name was Campbell, the Campbell Soup Company really belonged to her.

In 1971, Luella's fourth daughter, Beatrice gave birth to a son. This was the first grandchild born to one of Luella's daughters. He would become a special grandchild because he was born on Luella's son, Marion's birthday. The happiness over her new grandchild was soon abated however, because with school integration, many Black teachers became unemployed. Her daughter Ruby's contract with the Macon County Board of Education was not renewed for the school year 1971-1972. Luella encouraged her to join her two sisters in Syracuse to look for employment there. Therefore, in late summer 1971, Ruby traveled to Syracuse.

During the last month of the year in 1971, Luella's brother-in-law Paten died. That was somewhat of a setback for the entire Beal family. Paten possessed great humanity and was a magnanimous family man, uncle, brother-in-law, and brother.

All his children, his brothers' and sisters' children thought that he could move mountains and so did his wife and sister-in-law, Luella. Luella and Paten both shared very similar temperaments and were highly spiritual. They both possessed unyielding wisdom and were not arrogant individuals. Luella and Paten both loved children but did not play with children and demanded and received a high degree of reverence from them.

In 1972, Luella's youngest daughter was the first daughter to get married. She gave Vesta a large wedding after she secured a promise from her that she would complete her college education. Therefore, on a hot evening in August, the entire Beal clan gathered in Newtown for the first wedding of one of the Beal girls.

Figure 33: Luella's youngest daughter's wedding

CHAPTER 10 ~ Return to Parenting – Grandchildren - 1970-1979

The following year, Patience gave birth to her 12th child, a girl who was named Jacquelyn, aka Jackie. She probably was named for Jacqueline Kennedy because before her, there was no other female in the immediate or extended family named Jacqueline.

Unfortunately, Jackie did not get the opportunity to bond with or grow up knowing her mother. Technically, Jackie was Patience's 13th child because she gave birth to a stillborn child after the death of her first born, Joseph. Patience died when Jackie was only nine months old.

God provided Luella with a test of her conviction that she would not raise any grandchildren unless the mother died. Well, Patience died and left eleven children all under the age of eighteen. Four of these children were girls. The oldest child was sixteen years old. Three of the children were already living with Luella: Nathaniel who moved in years earlier, Jackie and Avis (Niecey).

Six months after the death of her daughter-in-law, Patience, Luella's middle daughter Mary decided to journey to the African continent for an indefinite stay. Luella as the supportive mother that she had always been did not discourage her daughter but told her to go with God's blessing and always put God first. However, Luella's oldest brother was not as supportive. Following the death of her daughter-in-law Patience, and her daughter Mary's journey to Africa, two of her brothers died. Her oldest brother, Buck died in Atlanta. It appeared that he had taken care of all the business affairs and left his wife, Emma Rosa, of fifty years without an anchor. Therefore, Emma Rosa turned to her sister-in-law, Luella for support and assistance. The family's industrious giant stepped up to the ship's stern and guided the family through yet another storm.

However, Luella did not realize that another storm was on the horizon, because a few weeks later, her brother Charlie died. Charlie was Luella's competitor, accomplice, and nemesis during their childhood days. However, as they matured into adults, he was one of her biggest supporters. Charlie lived most of his adult life in Hollywood, Florida where he died in July 1974.

Unlike Luella's sister-in-law Emma Rosa, Charlie's wife had several children from a previous marriage who provided her assistance and support. Daisy understood the closeness of the Campbell children, so she deferred to them concerning Charlie's final funeral arrangements. Part of the Campbell clan tradition was to bury loved ones amongst their earlier deceased family members. Therefore, Richard, Charlie, Buck were all buried in Cordele.

Figure 34: Luella's two oldest brothers

Two of Luella's daughters offered to assist in raising Happy's younger children; however, their father, Luella's second oldest son, James (Happy) insisted that he wanted his children raised together. As providence would have it, this matter was taken out of his hands less than four years later.

Since Happy was a womanizer, one of his cohorts in a jealous rage called child welfare and informed them that the children were being neglected and left home alone unsupervised. This occurred after the oldest daughter graduated from high school and moved out of state. Once social welfare initiated a case, they proposed to send the underage children to foster home care. But Luella stepped in and said that "The state was not scattering my grandkids throughout the state, I appeal to become their legal guardian". Luella became guardian of eight grandchildren.

By the end of 1976, Luella at almost 67 years of age, became a single foster parent to eight grandchildren. She orchestrated the enclosing of the carport on her home to add a room and a bathroom for the boys. At that time, Luella was still providing care for her Aunt Eva and provided occasional refuge for her brother John. Those responsibilities were becoming overwhelming because unlike her childbearing experience where she basically spaced her children, Happy and Patience's children were born on average thirteen months apart.

When the burden of raising small children seemed too much for Luella, she reached out to her two oldest living daughters for assistance. Luella also received support from her youngest daughter and her granddaughter Bertha. Luella requested that her daughter Mary return home from Africa to assist her with raising her grandchildren. She asked her daughter Ruby to assist her oldest granddaughter, Fannie, with continuing her education and/or finding a job in Syracuse. By 1976, Fannie was already living in Syracuse and her next oldest granddaughter was preparing to graduate from high school.

Since none of Luella's daughters was residing with her or nearby, she trained her granddaughter Niecey in domestic science and care giving duties. Niecey served as Luella's helper and gradually became the family's primary cook.

Luella had some high standards for her children and grandchildren. She placed God first in her life and clearly demonstrated her beliefs by her daily living. It could be honestly said that Luella's life was patterned after the Bible in so many ways. Luella knew that there were things and situations that she could not control for her children and grandchildren; however, she knew that it was her responsibility to teach them right from wrong. Luella welcomed her children's friends with open arms, but like her children, they had to respect her house rules. All of children, grandchildren, great-grandchildren and nieces and nephews knew that they could not bring a member of the opposite sex to Luella's house and expect to sleep in the same bed. Luella simply would not tolerate promiscuous behavior in her house.

Years later, her youngest son Jimmy's friend commented: "Luella applied the same rules to her children's friends that she applied to her own children". Merilyn Tickles, a friend of Luella's youngest son provided the following comments about her. Merilyn related, "This happened many years ago. Jimmy and I were visiting Cordele with the intention of driving back home later that day. So, the day turned into night we were over at his mom's house. Jimmy decided to stay in Cordele. I shared this with Mrs. Beal "She asked me where was I going to sleep"? Merilyn got the message, "Mrs. Luella Beal did not allow unmarried couples to sleep together in her house". Merilyn witnessed the respect that is given to her by all her children, grandchildren, and great grandchildren. She learned that quality is taught and expected by all that encounter Mrs. Beal. Merilyn stated, "Mrs. Beal is a very warm and caring person that you can talk to and expect true advice from her."

Mary returned home from Africa in early 1977. She spent one month in Cordele before moving to Atlanta. She immediately found temporary employment in the Atlanta area. The temporary employment turned into full-time permanent employment and Mary invited two of Luella's grandsons to live with her by 1978. Mary continued to support and assisted her mother by acting as surrogate parent when Luella traveled out of town.

Luella maintained close personal contact with her oldest sister during her entire life. One of the reasons was because Josephine's children and especially her oldest daughter, Vesta was her friend and childhood playmate. Another reason was that Tallahassee was less than a three-hour drive by automobile, and during the forties and fifties there was a passenger train that operated between Cordele and Tallahassee. Another reason was because Josie's sons would often bring their children to Cordele to visit with their aunts. Although Josie, as she was fondly called by her siblings, had reached her late 80s, it was still somewhat of a shock when she died. Since their mother, Surena, lived to reach her 90s, it seemed that every female family member was expected to live at least as long.

During the latter part on the 1970s, Luella strengthened her friendship with two long-time acquaintances that possessed automobiles and could drive. Janet Pace retired from teaching school and she and Luella would travel throughout Southwest Georgia and North Florida. Janet Pace taught many of Luella's children and grandchildren during her teaching career. Janet's mother had shown high respect for Luella. Janet instructed Luella's children to call her Mama Pace outside of the classroom. The other acquaintance was more like a sister to Luella and had been a friend since their school days. Her name was Lucille Hargrove Dixon. Many people in Dooly, Crisp and Macon Counties knew her as Hon Dixon or Cilla Dixon. There were others, but these two individuals seemed to be Luella's soul mates.

Luella seemed to have had the respect and admiration of most of her sister-in-laws. She had two sister-in-laws that resided in the state of New Jersey, and they maintained contact through mail and telephone. After the death of Emma Rosa's sister in Macon County, Georgia, Luella invited her sister-in-law, Emma Rosa, to Cordele to live with her family. Luella's love for her deceased brother would not allow her to forsake his widow. Although Emma Rosa's personality was somewhat eccentric, Luella had a way of dealing with the most difficult personalities. Luella had the support of her children and grandchildren to assist her in providing care for her sister-in-law.

Figure 35: James "Happy", wife Patience and oldest granddaughter

Figure 36: Luella dancing with a hula hoop

Figure 37: Alexander Campbell

Figure 38: Richard Campbell

was John and Surena Campbell's third son and their sixth child. He married Nora Meadows and they lived most of their marriage life in Chattanooga Tennessee.

Figure 39: Charlie Campbell

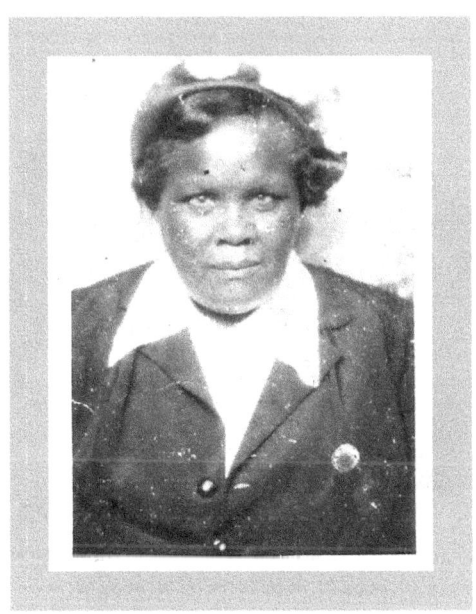

Figure 40: Eula Campbell McKenzie

Figure 41: Brooksie Campbell Lucas

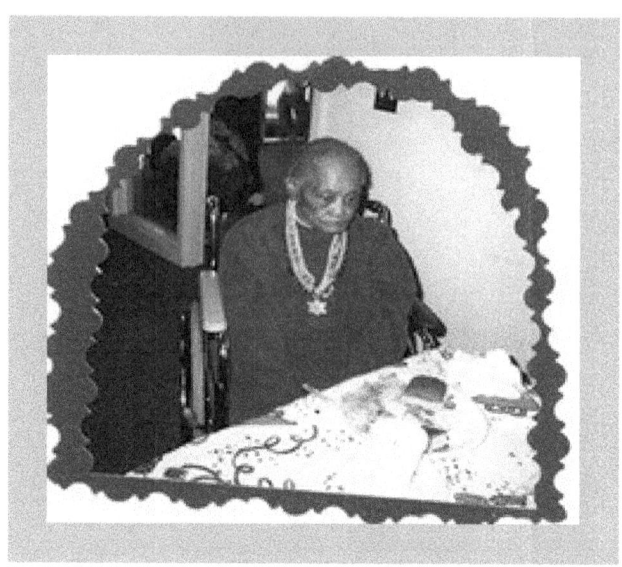

Figure 42: Seabright Seay Wiggins

Luella's first cousin noted for wearing her great-grandmother's beads.

Figure 43: Lucille Hargrove Dixon

Luella's lifetime friend at Luella's 85th Birthday celebration

CHAPTER 11 ~ Family Counselor and Hospice Caregiver 1970-1979

Luella probably felt like Mrs. Atlas (with the world on her shoulders) during the entire decade of the 1970s. She was there to support and comfort family members during bereavement of three loving and supportive brothers and one brother-in-law in the earlier part of that decade. She also witnessed the passing of several female members of her large extended family in the last half of that decade. It appeared that was when Luella became the super glue that held her large extended family together. Fortunately, she did not have to hold the family together alone, because she still had one older sister, one older brother and her youngest sister alive and mentally sharp to help her. However, Luella was still the most mobile and active of the four.

Even though she was James' widow, she had remained an integral part of the Beal extended family. When his oldest brother Frank died in the winter of 1976, she was unable to travel to New York. However, she encouraged her children living in upstate New York to attend Frank's funeral.

The first female family member's death in that decade from the Fields-Massey lineage was its matriarch Victoria Massey Toomer. Aunt Vic died shortly after she celebrated a century of life on earth. Naturally, Luella traveled to Savannah to sympathize with and support her cousins during that bereavement.

Less than two years later, Luella's oldest sister, Josephine died in Tallahassee, Florida. Luella having attained the Aquarian initiation at birth felt that one must return to life much of what it gathered along the way. She was a puzzle to friends and family: young at heart, possessed wisdom, liberal to an extent and sometimes exhibited unconventional behavior.

Her oldest living son, Happy, often recalled an incident that he witnessed as a youth. "I saw Mama, shoot a hawk in midair because the hawk was attempting to steal one of her chickens." To the hawk's disadvantage, she was a deadly force to reckon with because when the buck shot hit, the hawk dropped the chicken to the ground. Luella not only could handle a shotgun and rifle, but she had a deadly aim with a pistol. She could have easily earned a sharpshooter medal of honor.

Other times she appeared to be a psychic because of her keen intuitive mind which led her children to believe that she had eyes both in the front and back of her head. Her spirit appeared to exist in the world of the future. Two of her children frequently commented that Luella was born before her time. Little did they know that she simply exemplified strong characteristics of an Aquarian and a true Christian. The Aquarian positive qualities are individuality, friendliness, vision, genius, ingeniousness, and tolerance. As an Aquarian, Luella's love was detached, unselfish and idealistic and viewed as a oneness which she considered eternal.

As stated earlier, Luella was born into a loving, close-knit family that embodied the best of Native American and African traditions and principles. Many African tribes refer to female offspring of sisters by blood as belonging to each sister. Each sister would be identified in order by her age and name. The oldest sister was called Big Mama; the youngest sister was called Little Mama and the sister that gave birth to the child was called Mama.

To a large extent, Luella's large extended family followed those traditions. The practice of those traditions could be clearly seen in the interactions of Luella with her maternal aunts and their daughters and the interactions she had with her own sisters' children.

When Luella asked her Aunt Vic and her first cousin Rosa for assistance with accommodations for a third daughter to enroll at Savannah State College, it was provided without hesitation. Aunt Vic had four daughters, but none of them bore any daughters. Rosa had one adopted son, Annie had two sons and Adel and Agnes did not have any children: therefore, Luella's girls were welcomed into the home on East Anderson Street in Savannah.

Luella used her trips to Savannah to maintain close contact with her aunt and cousins. In addition to Aunt Vic and her daughters, Luella had another first cousin who was a resident of Savannah. J. Paul Salmon was the youngest son of her Aunt Luella and Uncle Texas Salmon.

CHAPTER 12 ~ Accomplishments of the Eighties: Traveling, Community Organizing 1980- 1989

Luella had been the primary caregiver for her Aunt Eva for almost 20 years when she died of heart failure in 1980. Her Aunt Eva was not a difficult person to care for, however, she often interfered when Luella attempted to discipline misbehaving children.

Many of Luella's grandchildren sought out Aunt Eva when Luella was preparing to administer punishment with a switch or a belt. Aunt Eva had a habit of talking out loud to herself. However, when it came to whipping children, she spoke directly to the individual administering the whipping. Usually, the only time that one heard her swear was when she heard a child crying.

Luella seemed to have understood her aunt and told her children and grandchildren that Aunt Eva was a caregiver for children who were born in the state mental hospital at Milledgeville, where she was a resident for approximately 25 years.

During many of Aunt Eva's tirades, she would mention many of her ancestors by name. Luella often found herself explaining to her children and grandchildren about the relationship of those individuals discussed in Aunt Eva's one-way conversations.

After Aunt Eva died, Luella's second youngest granddaughter, Niecey became her younger siblings' savior in many cases from Luella's switches. A plum tree and another evergreen shrub grew in Luella's backyard that produced great switches. Niecey became a great cook and housekeeper while living with her grandmother, Luella. She earned her grandmother's trust and confidence by making sound decisions and by not rebelling when she was told "no."

The year after Aunt Eva died, Luella's sister-in-law Mary died in Detroit. It was the first time she had traveled unaccompanied by airplane without one of her children or grandchildren. She was accompanied by Fred, a nephew by marriage.

Luella remained in Detroit for several days after her sister-in-law's funeral and visited with her first cousin, Ruby Lester Casey. Although Luella went to Detroit for a sad occasion, by extending her visit, she received a southern form of hospitality from her in-laws and other relatives. Luella was impressed by her visit to Canada. That was the first and only time that Luella traveled outside the United States.

On Halloween, in 1981, Luella's youngest son Jimmy received second and third degree burns over one-third of his body. The burns were caused from gasoline that ignited while he was working on his van. He recalls "When I awoke the next morning in the intensive care ward of St. Joseph's Hospital, the first and only person I saw was my mama." Luella remained in Atlanta and constantly by his bed for over six weeks.

When she said to him on the December 21st, "Baby, I have to leave you to go home to take care of some of personal business," Jimmy said, "I wanted to cry." It was as if she had talked (prayed) the fire out of his body, because two days later he was released to go home to complete his recuperation.

Luella could often be heard singing another one of her favorite hymns:

"I Must Tell Jesus" By Elisha Hoffman.

*I must tell Jesus all my trials, I cannot bear these
Burdens alone, In my distress He kindly will help me,
He ever loves and cares for His own.
I must tell Jesus! I must tell Jesus! I cannot bear my
Burdens alone; I must tell Jesus! I must tell Jesus!
Jesus can help me, Jesus alone.*

*I must tell Jesus all my troubles, He is a kind, compassionate
Friend, If I but ask Him, He will deliver, Make of my troubles
quickly an end. I must tell Jesus! I must tell Jesus! I cannot bear my
Burdens alone; I must tell Jesus! I must tell Jesus!
Jesus can help me, Jesus alone.*

In the fall of 1982, Luella's third born child, Marion was diagnosed with terminal stomach cancer. He returned to Cordele from south Florida and resided with Luella's youngest daughter, Vesta. Less than three months after his return, he succumbed to cancer on Christmas Eve of that year.

Luella as a force to reckon with surfaced again. Marion was estranged from his wife during the last six months of his life. However, when she learned of his death, she came to Cordele and announced that she was going to take her husband back to Fort Lauderdale. Luella adamantly stated in a no nonsense tone, "Over my dead body."

Luella was not an individual who took the law in her own hands, therefore, early the next business day, she with four of her children sat in a lawyer's office to discuss the immediate family's plan of action. The family had long known that when it came to matters pertaining to her children and respect, Luella could become an unleashed force to reckon with.

Luella's daughter-in-law, Maude learned that she was a force to reckon with and returned to Fort Lauderdale prior to the funeral. Although, the Christmas of 1982 was a sad time for Luella and her family, New Year's Eve was a time to celebrate. Luella was blessed with her first great-granddaughter on that day. She was also blessed with her second great-grandson earlier that month.

During the 1980s, Luella saw five of her grandchildren complete their high school education. When Avis, aka Niecey, graduated from high school in 1982, Luella did not attempt to dissuade her from migrating to upstate New York with her older sister and two aunts.

She was pleased with her grandchildren because none of them engaged in any serious infractions of established laws during their teenage years. Also none of her daughters or granddaughters became teenage unwed mothers. Luella encouraged Niecey to go to Syracuse to assist Luella's oldest granddaughter with her newborn baby girl.

Figure 44: Luella at granddaughter's wedding in 1984, Syracuse, NY

Luella's children learned many of her likes and dislikes simply by being in her presence. The death of a beloved and highly respected educator, Mr. Hiwarden Just, in 1984 revealed Luella's views on cremation. Although she had known others whose final remains were cremated, none of those individuals was as emotionally connected as she and Mr. Just.

Mr. Just had taught several of her children and grandchildren. They had formed a bond in the late 1950s, and it continued to cement for approximately twenty-five years.

It was during this time that she instructed her children and grandchildren that if she preceded them in death, they were not to have her body cremated. It was also around that same time when Luella had her tomb prepared at the Macedonia Baptist Church Cemetery at Drayton. Her tomb is situated between two of her deceased children.

In 1985, Luella's children attempted to give her a surprise 75th birthday party. However, it was not a surprise because one of the invitees could not read and asked mom to read his mail for him. Her children did not know that for almost thirty years she had performed that function for neighbors who could not read.

Luella kept a lot of things to herself and did not let the family know until after the event that she had inadvertently learned about the surprise party. One of her strong character traits was not to deliberately embarrass anyone. She was noted for taking individuals aside or behind closed doors and giving them a piece of her mind. Many times, Luella's lectures were worse than the sting of switches.

Luella was known amongst her children, grandchildren, and great-grandchildren for her faith in God, her firmness concerning obedience and her tough love. She was also known for showing compassion for neighbors, friends, and animals.

Luella displayed some of her tough love to her oldest living child when he was incarcerated for delinquent child support. Luella often told her children, "I will not lie on you, I will not lie for you, and if you make your bed hard, you will sleep on it." She even visited him once or twice while he served a short time in prison for delinquent child support payments. Instead of compromising her values, she solicited help from family and removed the child support order and governmental involvement in caring for her grandchildren. Luella maintained that regardless of one of her children's behaviors, they would always be her child. She further stated, "I will love each with a mother's love, however, I will be highly disappointed by unaccepted behavior, because I taught you all better."

When Luella was seventy-six years old, she displayed her tough love again by carrying through with her decision to send her youngest granddaughter to Syracuse. She told her oldest daughter Ruby, "It is time for me to send Jackie to you because a 76-year-old grandmother and a 14-year-old granddaughter do not mix."

During the late 1970s and early 1980s, Luella decided to raise a rare breed of chickens (Red Cochin Bantam). Her children and grandchildren often laughed and commented about the physical characteristics of those fowl. Because feathers grew from the crown of the chickens' head to their claws, the children nicknamed them "boot legged chickens"; however, it did not phase Luella, because she would comment, "I will see how you act when they are cooked and on the table."

CHAPTER 13 ~ Refuge & Childcare, Missionary - 1990-1999

Luella's daughter, Mary, accepted another overseas work assignment in early 1991. This time it was with the with the Department of the Army in Europe. Although Mary had accepted the appointment several months earlier, her departure was somewhat stressful for her mother because Mary departed three weeks after the death and burial of Luella's last living brother, John. The impact of Mary's departure was softened by her granddaughter Jackie's decision to return to the south to attend college about forty miles from her grandmother. Luella's earlier display of tough love and wisdom enabled Jackie to leave the small town of Cordele and excel in sports and academics in Syracuse. Jackie lettered in track and field sports prior to graduating high school.

Luella was beginning to suffer from the empty nest syndrome in the early to mid-1990s. All eight grandchildren that she raised were either married, in college and/or had moved into homes of their own. Jackie's youngest brother, Scottye graduated from high school in 1988 and moved to the state capitol with an older brother. Herman and Donald both remained in Cordele and bought homes of their own.

Luella was able to spend a lot of quality time with her youngest granddaughter during the decade of the 1990s. Jackie eventually left college early and returned to Cordele where she obtained work at a local nursing home.

Since Jackie was raised by her grandmother, Luella, from nine months of life until middle school and beyond, they had developed a special bond over the years. Their relationship became even closer because Jackie would drive her grandmother to the nursing home to visit many of her friends.

Luella loved having someone in the house with her because she enjoyed taking care of people and doing for others. Jackie improved her cooking and baking skills during that time, and she made her grandmother very proud.

The Beal clan continued to produce offspring during the 1990s. There were eighteen great-grandchildren borne to Luella's grandchildren during the 1980s and 1990s. She maintained a vegetable garden in her back yard and owned two large food freezers. One of the large food freezers was in the storage house in the backyard. It served the same purposes as the old smokehouse when she lived on the farm.

Figure 45: Luella's youngest granddaughter's high school graduation

Although food was preserved through a different process, the storage house also contained canned fruit and vegetable preserves, jellies, and pickles and pecans. There was always room in Luella's house and plenty of food to feed all her family and others.

Luella was still very active in the 1990s and many of her older great-grandchildren experienced her discipline when they appeared not to heed her verbal guidance and warnings. Several of these great-grandchildren have recalled during family gatherings the spankings (whippings) they received when they broke her chair swing that was in her front yard. They did not fear their great-grandmother because they knew she had their best interest at heart and would cook great meals, bake cakes and cookies for them.

At the age of eighty-six Luella was brave enough to take a road trip to upstate New York in the middle of winter with her daughter Mary. They stopped over at her granddaughter's house in Virginia both on their trip to upstate New York and on their return trip to Georgia. It was amazing that in the middle of February, they did not encounter any snow during their week's stay until the day of their departure from Syracuse.

The purpose of the trip was to visit a great-granddaughter who was named in honor of Luella's oldest daughter, Christine, and her mother, Surena. Naturally, since she was so close to Rochester, she visited her youngest sister, Brooksie. Later in the spring of that year, Luella's oldest living sister, Julia died at ninety-nine years and ten months.

Luella, the family's super glue, would not delay in Cordele by waiting on children or grandchildren. She and a church member boarded a Greyhound bus and traveled to Chattanooga to support and take care of the family there. When Luella's great-niece, Chandra asked, "Aunt Luella, who brought you to Chattanooga?" Luella responded, "They were moving to slow, I had to get here to take care of you all."

All of Luella's great-nieces and nephews were grown and some had children of their own. However, Julia's death made Luella the oldest family member, and she assumed the role as matriarch of her large extended family with dignity and confidence. She made a long-lasting impression on her great-niece Chandra.

During the mid-1990s descendants of Luella's oldest sister, Josephine planned and coordinated the first organized family reunion which was held in Tallahassee, Florida (1994).

Figure 46: Luella with two of her nieces, Rena and Vesta in Tallahassee, Florida

The following year, the second family reunion was coordinated and hosted by Luella and her offspring in Cordele, Georgia (1995). During the business meeting at that family reunion, the group voted that they would conduct the family reunion every two years. The third family reunion was hosted in Fort Lauderdale, Florida by Luella's late sister, Eula's offspring (1997).

The fourth family reunion was held in Savannah, Georgia and hosted by Luella's offspring and her first cousin Paul's offspring (1999). During the family business meeting a question was raised about the name of the family reunion. It was recommended that the family reunion name change be voted on at the next reunion in the year 2001.

The reunion in 2001 was held in Chattanooga, Tennessee and hosted by Luella's sister, Julia's offspring. Luella and her sister Brooksie were the reservoir for the Fields, Massey, Campbell, and Lamb history. In that year, both had very sharp minds and their memories were excellent.

Although, Brooksie, did not travel to the reunion, Luella attended and was very vocal about changing the name to be all inclusive of her great-grandmother's people. The family voted to change the name from Campbell-Lamb to Fields, Massey, Campbell, and Lamb Family Reunion.

Figure 17: Luella's oldest great-granddaughter high school graduation

During 1998, Jackie decided to open a home daycare and learning center in the wing of Luella's house that once was the quarters for Jackie's brothers. She named her new business "Patience Home Daycare & Learning Center."

Figure 48- Luella's Nigerian Family 1

Her slogan was "A place your child can call home," and it offers a fun-filled learning environment. One might say this was right up Luella's alley, meaning that when it came to the care and training of children, her home was the place to be.

Figure 49: Luella's great-grandson high school graduation

Mary returned home from her European assignment in 1997; and would drive Luella on visits to Florida and Savannah during the late 1990s. Whenever and wherever Luella visited, she often knew of other extended family members living in the vicinity and would visit with them also.

During one visit to Orlando, Florida, she reconnected with one of her first cousins who shares her maternal grandmother's name. During her visits to Savannah, Georgia she connected with her Aunt Luella's son Paul and Aunt Vic's grandson Leroy. Therefore, through Luella's family connections, participation in the Fields, Massey, Campbell, and Lamb Family Reunion strengthened.

Luella was also active as a missionary sister at Macedonia Baptist Church in Drayton, Georgia. She continued to participate and support the church even though she had not been accorded the official title and recognition as "Mother of the Church" when she became the oldest living active female member. Church members who had grown up in the church personally acknowledged her as Mother Beal. That seemed to lessen the sting of church leaders diverting from long standing tradition in the designation of individuals to positions in the church.

Luella, along with two other female church members attended church conferences throughout Southwest Georgia as representatives from Macedonia. At one church conference in Americus, Georgia, Luella was approached by a woman who introduced herself as Francis Perry Williams. Mrs. Williams explained to Luella that her late daughter, Betty Jean was a friend of Luella's daughter Mary. She went on to explain to Luella that when her daughter Betty Jean died, Mary provided her invaluable and unforgettable assistance during her bereavement.

Over the years, they would look for each other at church conferences. Occasionally, when Mary visited her mother in Cordele, they would ride to Americus to check on Mrs. Williams.

Figure 50 Macedonia Baptist Church (founded in 1870)

CHAPTER 14 ~ The Sage of the Family and Community 2000-2009

According to Luella, *"there are four secrets to staying young, being happy, and achieving success. You must laugh and find humor every day. You got to have a dream. When you lose your dreams, you die. Anybody can grow older. Just keep on saying good morning. That does not take any talent or ability. "The idea is to grow up by always finding opportunity in change. Have no regrets. The only people who fear death are those with regrets."*

Except for relatives and a childhood classmate, Luella maintained friendships with people younger than herself. She told one of her daughters that all her older friends either were in the nursing home or in the cemetery. Luella visited nursing homes often to give younger friends and family members encouragement and support. Although she had developed arthritis in her knees, she did not stop traveling to family reunions and other family events. Luella's performance over the decades can be compared to the Timex's slogan, "She takes a licking, but she keeps on ticking." The family caravanned to upstate New York for the high school graduation of her oldest great-granddaughter, Avanese.

Upon their arrival in Syracuse, Luella learned that her daughter, Beatrice was hospitalized. Beatrice's physicians discovered she had pancreatic cancer and planned surgery shortly after Luella's return to Cordele.

Once Beatrice's physicians in upstate New York released her, she moved back to Cordele and resided with Luella's youngest daughter, Vesta. Luella was saddened for her daughter's medical condition; however, she was relieved that she was nearby so she could check on her more frequently.

After about fifteen months of battling the pancreatic cancer in her body, Beatrice succumbed to this fatal illness. That happened less than a month before the wedding of Luella's youngest granddaughter, Jackie.

In the year 2003, Luella lost two more family members; both of whom were very close to her. They were Luella's step-mother-in-law, Magnolia (96) and a maternal first cousin, Seabright (89). That represented half of Luella's contemporary companionships in the local area.

Luella's father-in-law married Magnolia West and moved her to the Old Leonard Estate during the early 1940s. Hence, they had shared approximately sixty years of companionship. Luella and Seabright were like sisters. Magnolia assisted Luella during the birth of her last seven children. Magnolia's importance to Luella and other family members was more apparent because for a long time she was the only female who could drive a car or a truck on the farm. Not only could she drive an automobile, but she was an excellent seamstress, a great cook, and an admirable hostess. She was a God-fearing woman and a very hard worker. Since Magnolia was only three years older than Luella, they seemed to have had the same shared philosophy about life, raising children, reverence for God and the same work ethics.

Therefore, Magnolia's death probably had a more emotional impact on Luella than her first cousin. Although Luella and her first cousin, Seabright's relationship was very close, they did not share the daily routines of work, play, caring and sharing that Luella and Magnolia did for more than sixty years. It is unknown whether the stress of Magnolia's death brought on what physicians believed to have been a mini stroke in Luella in May of 2003.

Luella's fortitude and determination that she would not become a burden for others was witnessed during her rehabilitation. Until that episode, she had spent only three days in a hospital bed because of her own illness or sickness. Every one of her ten children was born at home with a midwife. Luella breastfed nine of the ten children.

She was assigned to a rehabilitation facility in Sumter County, about thirty-five miles from her home. Luella did not like being away from home and fussed, but in the end, she realized the fastest way to return to her home was to buckle down and perform the therapeutic exercises. Therefore, at the age of ninety-three, she became a good patient and was discharged in less than two weeks. When she entered the rehabilitation facility, she could neither stand nor walk unassisted. However, in less than two weeks, she could walk with the aid of a walker and was discharged with follow-up in-home therapy.

The family also believed that because the Beal's were hosting the first family reunion with their new name in Luella's adopted hometown, she would rise to the occasion and not disappoint them.

Luella attended the weddings for her youngest granddaughter and youngest grandson that she raised. She traveled to Virginia and upstate New York for great-grandchildren's high school graduations. Several years later, she also attended her oldest great-granddaughter's wedding in the state's capital.

The Fields, Massey, Campbell, and Lamb Family Reunion held in 2003 was a resounding success. The main reason it was so successful was attributed to Luella's eyesight and memory and her youngest sister, Brooksie being back in Cordele.

Mary, who resided in the Savannah, Georgia metropolitan area, attended Jerusalem Baptist Church in Groveland the Sunday following the family reunion in Chattanooga. Mary heard someone call the name Carolyn Fields, and Mary asked the person sitting on the pew next to her to point out Carolyn Fields.

Mary was informed that Carolyn was not present in church that day, but the next Sunday, Mary was approached by a lady who introduced herself as Carolyn Fields. Mary asked Carolyn, "Is Fields your maiden name or are you married to a Fields?"

Carolyn responded, "I am married to Frank Fields." Mary provided Carolyn with her address and telephone number after explaining that she was a descendant of Frederick and Rachel Fields.

Several weeks later, Frank and his cousin Earl visited Mary with a photo album that had belonged to Earl's deceased mother. Earl's mother and Frank's father were sister and brother. Earl allowed Mary to scan the picture of a person Aunt Hattie Fields Carter thought to be Rachel.

Mary took her computer to Cordele and opened the file with the picture of the person believed to be Rachel without communicating any information to Luella.

Luella excitedly stated, "There is one of my grandmothers."

Mary regretted she did not have the camcorder on or had a witness present to observe her mother's reaction. The only other known person who was alive in 2003 and old enough to remember Rachel Fields was Luella's youngest sister Brooksie. However, Brooksie had lost her eyesight and could not see the image believed to be Rachel Fields.

Both of Luella's daughters, Ruby and Mary, recall that during their youth, Luella would proudly state, "When I was twelve years old, Great-grandmamma Rachel was one hundred and twelve years old. Carolyn, Frank, and his brother Jessie Fields attended the first Fields, Massey, Campbell, and Lamb Family Reunion held in Cordele, Georgia.

Luella always allowed her children and grandchildren a lot of latitude when it came to thinking for themselves. At the same time, she often quite verbally informed them, "You all do not think for me or order me around." She would accent that by placing her hands on her hips and stare them down as she said, "I am still the mama around here. If you make your bed hard, you must sleep in it." After her children and grandchildren became adults, she often could be heard praying for them and their safety.

Her middle daughter, Mary was the family's adventurer. In the fall of 2003, Mary accepted a six-month assignment in the war zone in the Middle East. Prior to Mary's departure to the Middle East, the family hired a young lady to spend nights with Luella so she would not be alone by herself in the house.

Unbeknown to Mary, her mother's stress over her departure was heightened daily based on news reports on CNN television. Finally, Luella's youngest daughter, Vesta called Mary and said, "You need to come home because your mother is stressing out over news reports on CNN, and she is glued to that television set."

After the death of her step-mother-in-law, Magnolia, Luella became the matriarch of her husband's family. She was the oldest of the three living widows of the Beal brothers. Annie Lou Harris Beal, Paten's widow, was the youngest of the sisters-in-law and Annie Mae Dowdell Beal, Willie Lee's widow, was about three years younger than Luella. Luella was highly respected by children, grandchildren, great-grandchildren, nieces, and nephews from both sides of her large extended family.

During the spring of 2005, Luella asked her daughter Mary to come get her. Mary did as her mother asked and moved her to the metropolitan Savannah area. After staying away from Cordele for two weeks, Luella became homesick and wanted to return. However, Mary explained that she could not in good consciousness allow her to return to Cordele and live in her house alone.

Luella fretted for a short time, but after she was assigned a young lady by the name of Cheron as her community nurse assistant, she appeared to become more comfortable in her new home. Mary only moved some of her clothes and her recliner to Pembroke; therefore, they made trips to Cordele almost twice each month.

Luella settled in with her routine in Southeast Bulloch County in the fall of 2005. Luella occasionally attended church at Jerusalem Baptist Church in Groveland with her daughter. She even got the opportunity to interact with Frank Fields and his family in Pembroke. Carolyn Fields accompanied Mary and Luella on a trip to Atlanta to witness Luella's oldest great-granddaughter's marriage in the fall of 2005. Luella is shown holding her youngest descendant in a photo taken at that wedding. She seemed to cherish holding her infant descendants and doing something special for all her grandchildren.

Since she was living close to Savannah, Luella wanted to visit her Aunt Vic's grave site. The first time her daughter took her to the Magnolia Memorial Gardens Cemetery she was not prepared for Luella's reaction to the fact that there was no headstone to mark Aunt Vic's grave site. She instructed Mary to make sure that her aunt had a headstone to mark her grave. Being the obedient daughter, Mary initiated plans to select and have a headstone installed to mark Aunt Vic's grave site. Once that project was completed, Luella was ready to return to Cordele.

In the last two months of the year 2006, Luella displayed a troubled spirit. She had trouble sleeping and would awaken her daughter, Mary, in the middle of the night by calling out the name of her youngest sister, Brooksie. After about two weeks of repetitive performance of that nature, Mary decided to move her mother back to Cordele.

Figure 51: Luella's oldest great-granddaughter wedding in Atlanta, Georgia

Mary appealed to the rest of her immediate family members with a two-tier plan of support for at least ninety days. She asked each sibling, niece, and nephew to commit to support either in service or financially. This enabled Luella to return to her home in Cordele and be near her last living sibling, Brooksie, during her transition from life in the flesh.

Brooksie's death was difficult because Luella had lost her last sibling and her best friend. She handled the bereavement with so much calm and resiliency. Luella was overheard saying, "My sister is in a better place because she was very sick."

Another reason she probably handled Brooksie's death with the calmness of a royal matriarch was due to the attention received from both her children and all her sisters' children. Luella became the mother/grandmother figure for the entire Campbell clan plus numerous others.

Although Brooksie was her lifetime friend, Luella had another friend who provided her more comfort than her sister. His name was Jesus. Throughout her life, Luella could be heard singing the old hymn, *What A Friend We Have in Jesus* by Joseph Scriven & Charles C. Converse.

What A Friend We Have in Jesus by Joseph Scriven & Charles C. Converse

What a Friend we have in Jesus, All our sins and griefs to bear!
What a privilege to carry Everything to God in prayer.
Oh what peace we often forfeit, Oh what needless pain we bear.
All because we do not carry Everything to God in prayer.
Have we trials and temptations? Is there trouble anywhere?
We should never be discouraged Take it to the Lord in prayer.

Can we find a friend so faithful Who will all our sorrows share?
Jesus knows our every weakness Take it to the Lord in prayer.

Are we weak and heavy laden, Cumbered with a load of care?
Precious Savior, still our refuge Take it to the Lord in prayer.
Do thy friends despise, forsake thee? Take it to the Lord in prayer.
In His arms He will take and shield thee Thou wilt find a solace there.

Figure 52: Family picture taken at oldest son's 75th Birthday celebration.

April 15, 2008

Figure 53: Five generations that attended the 2009 Fields, Massey Campbell, Lamb Family Reunion held in Cordele, Georgia.

Seated, Luella Campbell Beal, (Standing Center), son James "Happy", (Standing Left), Fannie Beal Harvey, oldest granddaughter, (Standing Right)

Avanese Harvey Taylor, oldest great-granddaughter, (In Fannie's Arms) Everett Charles Taylor, oldest great-great-grandson

CHAPTER 15 ~ Living Testimonies 2000-2010

In celebration of Luella's 99th birthday, many friends and family members were asked to respond to three questions: What is your most memorable comment(s) or expression(s) by Luella Campbell Beal? What impact, if any, did she have on your life, career, or occupation? What would you tell others, especially the younger generation about her? Their responses were both insightful and humorous and provided an impartial view of the sage of the community.

Dorothy Clark recalled some of many of Luella's comments to her over the years, "Girl, you need to go out the back door and get you a couple of bricks to put on the hem of that skirt," (referring to my dress). "I don't remember your name, but I know you haven't missed many meals," (referring to my weight). "You sho are one of them now (Beals) 'cause you loud just like them". "Now come help me to the bathroom."

Dorothy further stated that Luella inspired her to be a better and stronger mother and role model for her children and her grandchildren. In her professional life, Dorothy often referred to Luella to make points when she counseled residents.

She often referred to the fact that Luella raised her children (all successfully) and then she helped raised her grandchildren. Dorothy used Luella's experience to empower some of the grandparents she works with who become weary along the way. "Luella is such a strong matriarch," she said.

Dorothy said, "I often recite stories of how Luella overcame obstacles that were placed in her way." Dorothy also talked about Luella's strength of character, "You never have to second-guess Luella because she speaks her mind (never intentionally hurting anyone)." Dorothy said she uses Luella as an example of how a lifetime of mothering binds families forever.

Luella's niece, **Brooksie Hall**, also referred to her aunt's comments about her size, "You are not Lil' Brook anymore; you are BIG Brook now."

Brooksie also added, "I was always happy to see Aunt Luella come to Rochester to visit Mom, because it made Mom so happy, and it changed Mom's whole mood for the better."

Brooksie further stated, "I will tell anyone to look at Luella's accomplishments. When it comes to family, she was a good woman to raise two whole families, and not complain. Some women cannot bring up one.... God Bless Her! I am proud to be her niece."

"As her daughter, **Ruby Beal**, for sixty-four years, I can think of many things my mom, Luella has said. What can I record as a memorial comment, or should I say her mother wit of raising children? Two of mom's sayings is, "love is what it does," and "actions speak louder than words."

"As the sixth child born to James and Luella Campbell Beal, I am truly blessed to have her as my mother, and that she had a vision and a plan for me and my siblings. She truly believed in the value of a good education and wanted all her children to succeed. I was the first to graduate from high school, and my mother decided that I was going to college.

I graduated from A. S. Clark High School on June 3, 1963, and my father died on June 5, 1963. My mother decided I was going to Savannah State College. I was concerned about how we could afford it, but this woman of God relied upon her faith, family, and friends to put me through college.

I graduated from Savannah State in 1967, and because of the love, strength, and faith of my mother, I have had the pleasure to be an educator for almost forty years. As a teacher, I use many of my mom's sayings with my students. She is my inspiration and I share many stories about her views on discipline and her quips to gain their attention.

Mom was born before her time. This great woman could have been a doctor, psychologist, or a professional baseball pitcher if she had been born in the 1960s or 1970s when opportunities were opening for Blacks and women. She believes in discipline and often says, "Spare the rod and spoil the child."

She puts God first. This caring and compassionate person loves her family and puts the needs and care of her children and other family members before her own needs. 'Develop a relationship with God; love and respect all people; lend a helping hand whenever you can ', she says.

Luella's youngest granddaughter, **Jacqueline Beal**, recalled a conversation with her grandmother, in which she asked, "What's the matter, grandmamma?"

And her grandmother responded, "More the matter than you can scatter."

Jackie smiled and asked, "Grandmamma, repeat what you said."

Luella responded without a smile, "I said more to matter than you can scatter."

Jackie sighed and with a smile said, "I guess I will leave that alone." By growing up in Luella's house, Jackie was able to discern when her grandmother's comments were final.

Jackie also recalled the statement by her grandmother, "Early to bed early to rise makes you healthy, wealthy and wise." Jackie said, "I didn't know until I was an adult that statement was biblical."

Jackie said, "Grandmamma cared about her children and grandchildren getting an education. She knew it would make our lives easier than hers had been. The fact that I worked with children and enjoyed helping others probably came from her. I saw her helping friends, family and neighbors in need the best she could."

Jackie also said, "Grandma didn't play with kids; she believed wholeheartedly in 'spare the rod, spoil the child.' Children this day and age get away with murder, parents giving them things they have not worked for or earned. This has resulted in many ungrateful kids who think only of themselves. As grandmamma often taught us, 'it's not about you; it's about what you can do for someone else.'"

Dell Ford-Jordan, one of Luella's many foster daughters, most memorable expression from Mama Luella was her opinion on hygiene. Dell often visited Luella and inquired about her well-being. On one occasion, Dell asked Luella, "How are you doing?" Luella responded, "I'm doing fair. I am still able to do things for myself, important things that I can do well."

Dell asked, "What particular things are you talking about?"

Luella said, "Well, this morning I got up, said my prayers, brushed my teeth and washed down as far as possible. I then sat down and washed up as far as possible" – and then Luella paused and looked at Dell who was waiting patiently for her to finished. She looked at Dell and said with that dry humor only she can deliver, "And then I washed POSSIBLE."

Dell said "I roared with laughter. Mama Luella ended the conversation with the comment. 'It is good to be able to take care of your own hygiene.'"

Luella had a positive impact on Dell's life. She was there when Dell needed a listening ear, a loving smile, or an encouraging word. She was Dell's 'other' mother then and her 'only' mother after her birth mother died. Dell said, "Mama Luella was a friend to my birth mother when they visited Syracuse during the same time. They would often get together and talk about their children for hours. I love her very much."

Dell related that Mama Luella gives advice when needed and not needed. "That's her way and she will always tell you the truth." A famous saying of hers is 'In whatever you do in life always put God first.'

Luella's niece, **Elizabeth (Liz) Lucas**, affirmed her aunt's sense of humor by recalling one of Luella's favorite teasing statements to her, "If your head was a hog head, I could make a lot of Brunswick stew."

Liz applauded her Aunt Luella who showed through example what love she had for her family. Liz commented, "Aunt Luella made some real men and women out of the happy Beal boys and girls. Aunt Luella loved church and family and has 100 years to show for it."

Sulami Zakade Wulah, is one of Luella's grandsons who shared one of his grandmother's most memorable comments. Zakade, as he is called by the family, quoted his grandmother, "Baby, you can drive but you do know what the speed limit is."

He said he was speeding and immediately began driving at the posted speed limit. Zakade also stated, "Grandma's impact on my life was very inspirational because she always read the Bible and went to church. So, this gave me a spiritual foundation to keep me level in my walk-through life."

Zakade's response to the question: what would you tell younger generations about Luella Campbell Beal? He said, "I would tell anybody and everybody about my GRANDMOTHER. I would say let the life you live speak for you! That is what my grandmother did."

Robin Porter, one of Luella's many grandnieces, said. "I'm sorry to say I don't remember any specific conversations that I had with Aunt Luella. However, I have shared with my children and will share one day with my grandchildren how I feel that Aunt Luella is the glue that kept our family united. No matter what your relationship is to her, talking with her always makes you feel blessed that you are a part of her family."

Julia McKenzie Woods, another one of Luella's nieces, shares her memories of her aunt. "We would visit her during the summer, and she tried to teach me how to milk her cow. I was only six or seven years old and was afraid. But she taught my sister how to milk the cow, and she enjoyed it. I also remember Aunt Luella when she only had three boys and each summer, she asked me to stay with her because she did not have a girl. Later she had lots of girls. Aunt Luella would away thank God for everything!"

Bertha Beal Carnes, one of Luella's granddaughters said, "The most memorable thing about Grandmamma is the wisdom she gave me as a child and adult. My grandma gives you the truth if you like it or not and she is one who loves keeping family together.

"My husband and I had a problem and Grandma told me to take it back to the store. I listened to her, and things got better. Grandma played a very important part in my life by praying for me when I was doing my own things. Grandma has been serving God for a mighty long time. I believe her favorite scripture is the 23rd Psalms."

Bertha said that her advice to the younger generation is to listen to older adults who are doing God's work. She added, "Older adults have a lot of wisdom; and don't let bad company get you in trouble when you know better."

"Grandma used tell us, 'Watch the company you keep and do not let your good deeds be spoken with evil thoughts. An idle mind is the devil's workshop." So always try to do something good for people.' Grandma was always helping people in her home, church, and the community where she lived."

Avanese Taylor, Luella's oldest great-granddaughter traveled to Cordele shortly after her baby was born. Ava introduced her son, Everett Charles (E.C.) to his great-great grandmother, Luella, by saying, "Grandma, this is E.C., Fannie's grandson."

Luella responded, "Y'all trying to pull one over on Fannie; she doesn't have no grandchildren."

Ava said, "My most memorable moment was when Grandma asked if she could hold the baby." Ava contends that "Grandma Luella, is the epitome of what a strong Black woman is. She is the reason why we value our family so much. She is 100 years old and mighty fine. She always has a sense of humor and doesn't take any mess from anybody."

Ava's mother, Fannie Beal Harvey, shared the following quotes from her grandmother, "'Whatever you do, put God first in your life. Keep a job to take care of yourself and your family and teach your kids those same values.' Grandma would tell you like it was whether you liked it or not."

Vesta Beal Shephard, Luella's youngest daughter's most memorable comment from her mother was, "Show me the company you keep; and it will tell me who you are."

Vesta stated, "As a young lady I was not permitted to hang out in the night clubs or with friends who had babies before marriage, attending high school while pregnant, or who kept their babies. She believed if you hung with the crowd, you were doing the same thing they did. I was allowed to participate in all religious and school functions."

Vesta add, "Mom sort of shaped me into who she wanted me to be. I always thought I wanted to be a computer programmer. The only college that specialized in computer programming was in Atlanta, where I wanted to attend college."

Luella said to Vesta, "You are no different from your sisters; you will be going to Savannah State College. You will be living with our cousin Rosa Emerson. End of conversation." Vesta graduated in 1975 from what is now Savannah State University with a bachelor's degree in sociology. She has been doing medical social work since 1974.

Vesta said, "Never underestimate the strength of a true southern Black woman. Luella Beal has been a tower of strength for the family, church, and the community. She is ever so loving, very opinionated, has a superior sense of pride, a keen sense of humor and please remember she has the jazziest mouth in the South; you never have to second-guess her, she will always tell it like it is."

Terletha Louise McKenzie Wallace stated, "My Aunt Luella is a great aunt. She has been in my life as long as I can remember. When I used to go on vacation every year, I would go to Georgia. We would have a good time. We had to go to Drayton. She loved Drayton. When we would go to Byromville, she would have me go through the Drayton back road. It would be me, Aunt Luella, Baby James, and Pig (Shirley's nickname).

Aunt Luella has had a great impact on my life. I see myself in her. Our lives are somewhat alike, especially in raising our families. She is my favorite aunt. I would tell my children to try to be like Aunt Luella. She is a good person. She goes to church, loves everyone, and treats people good, gives respect and demands respect. They all know Aunt Luella. My brother Sonny, used to call me Luella."

Luella's neighbors, **Betty and Mulford Roberson** commented, "Mrs. Beal was and still is our inspiring neighbor and role model at age ninety-nine! Her comments that we remember best are those she made in earlier years when my husband Mulford and I were busy working and raising our children and had little time to visit. When my children played outside, sometimes Mrs. Beal and I held priceless conversations while watching them play. She shared wisdom and advice that I treasured.

"Mrs. Beal was and is still a strong woman of God. One bit of advice was, 'always put God first. Go to church and take your children to church.'

She also believed in, 'Remember the Sabbath Day and keep it Holy.' This she said means no cutting the lawn on Sunday, and no fishing on Sunday. She also practiced what she preached.

"Mrs. Beal stressed manners. She said, 'teach children manners so they will have respect for themselves and especially have respect for their elders.'

"I will tell the younger generation that if they could have a conversation with Mrs. Beal, it would be one of life's treasures. She has so much wisdom. She stressed education and worked hard to help educate her children, grandchildren, and great-grandchildren enabling them to become contributing citizens of the communities in which they live."

"Presently, Mrs. Beal is still in control and gives orders. When she rides by my home, and I go out to speak to her, she tells me, 'Go put your shoes on.' I respond, "Yes Ma'am." I go and put my shoes on!

"Above all, our community is blessed to have Mrs. Beal who is a marvelous example of God's love and who gives love and inspiring words of wisdom to anyone in her presence."

Another neighbor, **Mr. Henderson Dunn**, dictated the following comments. "I have never met such a nice, intelligent, and loving neighbor in my eighty-nine years of life. Our children ate together, played together, and had a good time. I remember when her husband passed, that she told me to be happy because her husband had gone home to rest with his Father in Heaven.

"Mrs. Beal was a Christian hearted woman and was good to listen to and helped me to raise my children. Anytime I asked for her help, she assisted me. It was the same with me and my wife. We watched over each other's family and prayed for our children to do well in life.

"By the help of the Lord, he heard our prayers. We have good, well-educated children and they love, with respect, the old and the young. I pray to the good Lord that they will live loving lives for our Father in Heaven.

"I would tell the younger generation, "As long as Mrs. Beal is up and able to talk with you, she will tell you to live a life that God will be well-pleased with. I hope my words will be on some young man, boy, or girl's heart and mind so they will live where God can use them, anywhere and anytime. I hope these words will lift some young man or woman."

Vesta Mae Lamb Dean commented, "I am the oldest living niece of Luella Beal. My mom, Josephine Campbell Lamb and she were sisters. Luella and I are just four years apart and played together when we were children. She has been a rock in my life, and I have always admired her for her strength, smartness, and motivation.

"She was very wise, and as we grew older, married and moved away from each other, we still kept in touch by telephone and visits. We would talk for hours sharing our family and religious experiences. Now, Luella is one hundred-plus years, with me on her heels. We are both ailing now, and our talks and visits have slowed considerably, but I still think of her as one of my favorite aunts...Aunt Luella, Aunt Luella, Aunt Luella...I dearly love you!"

CHAPTER 16 ~ One Hundredth Birthday Celebration February 13, 2010

Figure 54: Luella with her five living children on her 100th Birthday

February 13, 2010

Figure 55: Cake designed and made by Luella's brother-in-law, Paten's oldest granddaughter, B'Neika Johnson

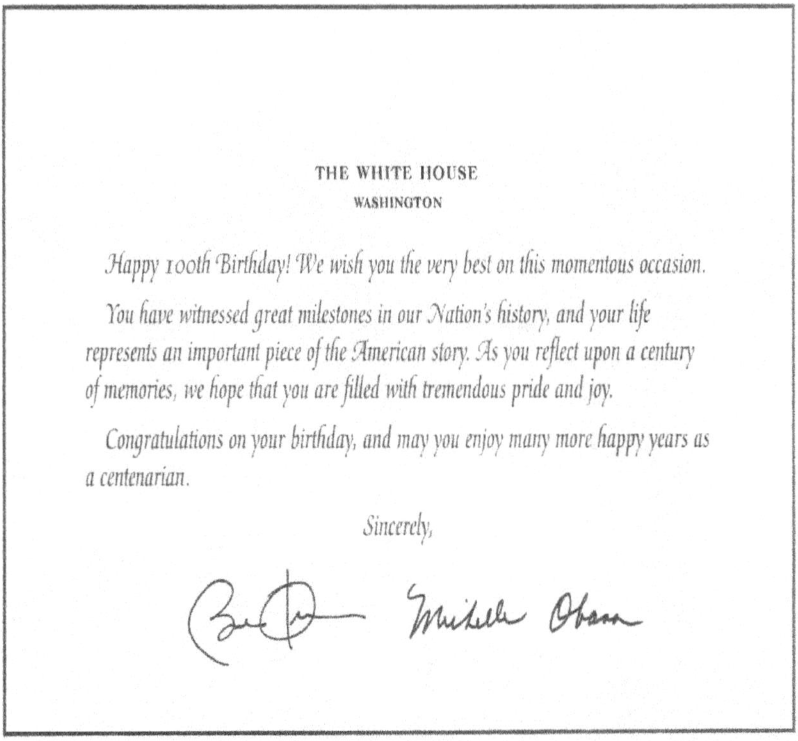

> THE WHITE HOUSE
> WASHINGTON
>
> *Happy 100th Birthday! We wish you the very best on this momentous occasion.*
>
> *You have witnessed great milestones in our Nation's history, and your life represents an important piece of the American story. As you reflect upon a century of memories, we hope that you are filled with tremendous pride and joy.*
>
> *Congratulations on your birthday, and may you enjoy many more happy years as a centenarian.*
>
> *Sincerely,*
>
> *Barack Obama   Michelle Obama*

Figure 56: Birthday wishes from The White House

PROCLAMATION
FOR
LUELLA CAMPBELL BEAL

WHEREAS, on this day, 13 February 2010, LUELLA CAMPBELL BEAL, observes a true milestone – she is celebrating her life at the century mark of one hundred years

WHEREAS, Luella Campbell Beal is a and has been a resident of Newtown in Crisp County, Georgia for more than fifty (50) years

WHEREAS, Ms. Beal has participated in many projects and initiatives in the Cordele Community. She has been a dedicated blood donor until she exceeded the age limitation

WHEREAS, Mrs. Beal is an active in her church, and as a parent and grandparent having served in various Parent Teacher Organization for more than forty (40) years;

WHEREAS, Mrs. Beal remains a civic minded individual and an advocate for discipline in the youth of our community.

WHEREAS, Mrs. Beal is loved by all who knows her and especially her immediate and extended family where she serves as a role model as well as others with whom she spends quality time.

NOW THEREFORE, the City of Cordele does hereby proclaim the 13th day of February 2010 as **LUELLA CAMPBELL BEAL** day as our awareness of her celebration of one hundred years, and to demonstrate community awareness and positive involvement of Cordele citizens;

This 2nd day of February 2010.

City of Cordele

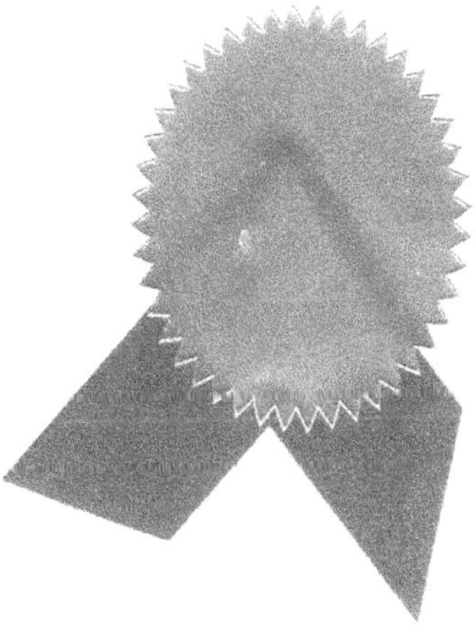

By _____
Zack H. Wade
Chairman, Cordele City Commission

Attest _____
Jean H. Burnette
City Manager

Figure 57 Proclamation for Luella Campbell Beal by Cordele, GA

STATE OF GEORGIA
COUNTY OF CRISP

A PROCLAMATION OF
LUELLA CAMPBELL BEAL'S DAY IN CRISP COUNTY

WHEREAS, LUELLA CAMPBELL BEAL has resided in the Newtown Community for over fifty years, actively participating in many community initiatives; and

WHEREAS, LUELLA CAMPBELL BEAL was a dedicated Blood Donor, giving the "Gift of Life" up until she exceeded the age limitation for donating; and

WHEREAS, LUELLA CAMPBELL BEAL is a civic minded citizen who advocates discipline in children was an active parent and grandparent in Parent Teachers Organizations for some forty years; and

WHEREAS, LUELLA CAMPBELL BEAL has always been an asset and role model for her immediate and extended family making a vocation of Mother, Care Giving and devoted Farmers wife; and

WHEREAS, LUELLA CAMPBELL BEAL has many interests including Family, Friends, Church, Community, Reading, Gardening and Traveling; and

WHEREAS, LUELLA CAMPBELL BEAL by her Quick Wit, Sharp Eyes and Warm Heart, has become a force to recon with in both family and community; and

WHEREAS, LUELLA CAMPBELL BEAL is a woman of many quotes, such as "Put God First", "Love is what it Does", "More to Matter than to Scatter" and A Hit Dog will Holler; and

WHEREAS, LUELLA CAMPBELL BEAL attributes her longevity to Diet, Nutrition, Attitude, Genetics and Spirituality.

NOW, THEREFORE, BE IT PROCLAIMED, that February 13, 2010, on the occasion of her 100th Birthday, be known as LUELLA CAMPBELL BEAL's Day in Crisp County.

This the 12th day of February 2010.

BOARD OF COMMISSIONERS OF CRISP COUNTY

Authur James Nance
Authur James Nance, Chairman

(Official Seal)

ATTEST: _Lester E. Crapse, Jr._
Lester E. Crapse, Jr., Administrator

Figure 58: Proclamation of Luella Campbell Beal Day in Crisp County

CHAPTER 17 ~ Epilogue

Centenarian – One Hundred and One Years

To provide a more in-depth summary of Luella's life, the author sought the assistance of the Internet, a communication-information source that Luella has been trying to comprehend, but just could not seem to grasp.

She analyzed a list of fifty-nine other individuals born in 1910. Fourteen of them were still alive at the time of the research, thirty-two died at the age of seventy or older; nine individuals died when they were under the age of seventy. Five of those under the age of seventy were in their mid to late 60s when they died. One individual died in her 40s and the three individuals who died in their 30s and 20s were gangsters and outlaws. This preliminary limited research provides an indication that lifestyle is a key factor in longevity.

Descendants of individuals born in the early 1900s will most likely glimpse some of their own life story as reflected in Luella's tale. Their ancestors probably shared things in common with Luella: a great sense of humor, a spiritual relationship with God, a self-sufficiency independent attitude, and a gregarious attitude about life and people.

Many people had the opportunity to meet Luella; however, not all of them experienced her quick and keen wit. Many of her caregivers, her children and grandchildren received a constant dose of her sharp wit. Luella's loyalty to family, friends, clubs, and her church are beyond reproach.

She is the embodiment of family super glue that cannot be purchased, duplicated, or copied. She was an original; she was solid as a rock, and she was the real thing.

The decade of Luella's birth was a period of great change for America and the world. It was during this decade that the United States was first considered a world leader. Many of the issues of that decade are ones we face today. The escalation of immigration and poverty, and a war remain issues one hundred years later. However, Luella weathered many changes, various wars, and countless personal misfortunes over one hundred years.

The great Walt Whitman wrote more than a century ago: "The genius of the United States is not best or most in its executives or legislatures, nor in its ambassadors, or authors or colleges, or churches, or parlors, nor even in its newspapers or investors, but always most in the common people."

However, Luella is not an ordinary commoner. She was a highly motivated commoner with royal expectations and an unyielding faith in God. Therefore, in death, she is a powerful force to reckon with!

After Luella's death, her daughters found several inspirational poems amongst her personal papers. There was much more to this spiritual force to reckon with and much of Luella's spiritually will be revealed in the sequel, *Help Me Cross Over from Earth to Heaven*. A few of those inspirational poems have been included in the sequel.

Thanks For Making My 100th Birthday A Most Memorable Occasion Gifts, Cards, Phone Calls & Your Presence

Luella Campbell Beal

Figure 59: Thank You Card from Luella

Figure 60: A Tribute to my mom on her Ninetieth Birthday

LUELLA CAMPBELL BEAL

If it had not been for you, I may have never known how truly strong and courageous a woman can be.

Because of your faith, your courage, your vision, and wisdom, I am the first college graduate in our family. You sent me to Savannah even though we did not have any money and Daddy had just died.

As I teach today, I thank God for blessing me with a mother who put her children first. You are truly a selfless person. Your quick wit has served me well. I often tell my students, my Mama says…"

I tell my students that you could have been a doctor or a baseball pitcher if you had been born in the 1960s instead of 1910. I still feel those cotton bolls you threw if you thought I was slackening up. Your homemade remedies and knowledge of herbs will never be forgotten. I cannot forget the castor oil.

Your journey has not been easy, but your faith has never faltered. You are the matriarch, the head mother. You are loving and caring ways have helped to keep this family together. Your tough love has guided me well. I do remember the whippings and read the Bible.

Because of your love and devotion to family, I am a member of a strong African American family today.

YOU ARE MY ROLE MODEL.

You are truly an inspiration.

Thank you, mama.

Love, Ruby

Figure 61: Living Testimony by Songwriters: Brownie, Matthew; Sapp, Marvin L

Lyrics to Never Would Have Made It:
Never would have made it, never could have made it, without you.
I would have lost it all, but now I see how you were there for me.

And I can say.
Never would have made it,
Never could have made it,
Without you

I would have lost it all,
But I know how I see how you were there for me and I can say
I am stronger, I am wiser, I am better,
much better,

When I look back over all you brought me through.
I can see that you were the one that I held on to
And I never
Chorus- Never would have made it

Oh I never could have made it

Centenarian – One Hundred Years and Counting

Chorus Never could have made it without you
Oh I would have lost it all, oh but now I see how you were there for me
I never
Chorus - Never would have made it

No, I never
Chorus - Never could have made it without you

I would have lost my mind a long time ago if it had not been for you.
I am stronger
Chorus – I am stronger

I am wiser
Chorus – I am wiser

Now I am better

Chorus – I am better

So much better
Chorus – I am better

Centenarian – One Hundred Years and Counting

I made it thru my storm and my test because you were there to carry me through my mess

I am stronger
Chorus – I am stronger
I am wiser
Chorus – I am wiser

I am better
Chorus – I am better

Anybody better
Chorus – I am better
I can stand here and tell you, I made it. Anybody out there that you made it
I am stronger
Chorus – I am stronger
I am wiser
Chorus – I am wiser

Centenarian – One Hundred Years and Counting

I am better
Chorus – I am better

Much better
Chorus – I am better
I made it, I made it, I made it, I made it, I made it, I made it, I made it, I made it
And I never would have made it
Chorus Never would have made it
Never could have made it

Chorus- Never could have made it without you
I would have lost my mind, I would have gave up, but you were right there, you were right there
I never
Chorus- Never would have made it
Oh, I never
Chorus - I never could have made it without you.
Someone need to testify next to them and tell them I am stronger, I am wiser, I am better, much better. When I look back over what he brought me thru. I realize that I made it because I had you to hold on to, now I am stronger, now I

Centenarian – One Hundred Years and Counting

am wiser, I am better, so much better. I made it. Is there anybody in this house other than me that can declare that you made it. Tell your neighbor, never would have made it. Never would have made it. Never could have made it. Never could have made it without you. Never would have made it. Never would have made it. Never could have made it. Never could have made it without you.

Figure 62: Matthew 6:19-34 (KJV)

19Lay not up for yourselves treasures upon earth, where moth and rust doth corrupt, and where thieves break through and steal:

20But layup for yourselves treasures in heaven, where neither moth nor rust doth corrupt, and where thieves do not break through nor steal:

21For where your treasure is, there will your heart be also.

22The light of the body is the eye: if therefore thine eye be single, thy whole body shall be full of light.

23But if thine eye be evil, thy whole body shall be full of darkness. If therefore the light that is in thee be darkness, how great is that darkness!

24No man can serve two masters: for either he will hate the one and love the other; or else he will hold to the one and despise the other. Ye cannot serve God and mammon.

25Therefore I say unto you, take no thought for your life, what ye shall eat, or what ye shall drink; nor yet for your body, what ye shall put on. Is not the life more than meat, and the body than raiment?

26Behold the fowls of the air: for they sow not, neither do they reap, nor gather into barns; yet your heavenly Father feedeth them. Are ye not much better than they?

27Which of you by taking thought can add one cubit unto his stature?

28And why take ye thought for raiment? Consider the lilies of the field, how they grow; they toil not, neither do they spin:

29And yet I say unto you, that even Solomon in all his glory was not arrayed like one of these.

30Wherefore, if God so clothe the grass of the field, which today is, and tomorrow is cast into the oven, shall he not much more clothe you, O ye of little faith?

31Therefore take no thought, saying, what shall we eat? or, what shall we drink? or, Wherewithal shall we be clothed? Centenarian –

32(For after all these things do the Gentiles seek:) for your heavenly Father knoweth that ye have need of all these things.

33But seek ye first the kingdom of God, and his righteousness; and all these things shall be added unto you.

34Take therefore no thought for the morrow: for the morrow shall take thought for the things of itself. Sufficient unto the day is the evil thereof.

The following quotes symbolize Luella Campbell Beal's life and her teaching:

"Home is the place where boys and girls first learn how to limit their wishes, abide by rules, and consider the rights and needs of others."
Sidonie Gruenberg

"Family life is full of major and minor crises -- the ups and downs of health, success and failure in career, marriage, and divorce -- and all kinds of characters. It is tied to places and events and histories. With all of these felt details, life etches itself into memory and personality. It's difficult to imagine anything more nourishing to the soul."
Thomas Moore

"Call it a clan, call it a network, call it a tribe, call it a family: Whatever you call it, whoever you are, you need one.".
Jane Howard

"Happiness is having a large, loving, caring, close-knit family in another city."
George Burns

"God could not be everywhere and therefore he made mothers."
Hebrew Proverb

"Educate and inform the whole mass of the people... They are the only sure reliance for the preservation of our liberty."
Thomas Jefferson

"Spread love everywhere you go: first, in your own home. Give love to your children, to a wife or husband, to a next-door neighbour."
Mother Teresa

"Life is an opportunity, benefit from it. Life is beauty, admire it. Life is bliss, taste it. Life is a dream, realize it. Life is a challenge, meet it. Life is a duty, complete it. Life is a game, play it. Life is a promise, fulfill it. Life is sorrow, overcome it. Life is a song, sing it. Life is a struggle, accept it. Life is a tragedy, confront it. Life is an adventure, dare it. Life is luck, make it. Life is too precious, do not destroy it. Life is life, fight for it."
Mother Teresa

"Govern a family as you would cook a small fish - very gently."
Chinese Proverb

"To nourish children and raise them against odds is in any time, any place, more valuable than to fix bolts in cars or design nuclear weapons."
Marilyn French

"In each family a story is playing itself out, and each family's story embodies its hope and despair."
Auguste Napier

"In every conceivable manner, the family is link to our past, bridge to our future."
- Alex Haley

"Perhaps the greatest social service that can be rendered by anybody to this country and to mankind is to bring up a family."
George Bernard Shaw

Centenarian

Sources

I am grateful to my maternal ancestors for having preserved so much of the family heritage. I am even more appreciative that they shared information with members of the family's younger generation. More importantly, older family members enhanced education. They left a legacy of educational expectations for younger members, family photos, and other artifacts along with strong spiritual beliefs.

Because of the family spirituality, daily Biblical teachings were used to train and educate most family members. The Bible itself was used to record key dates and events in the lives of family members. A family's personal Bible contained information on family genealogy, births, marriages, divorces, remarriages, and deaths.

My maternal ancestors possessed genetics that was passed down through DNA that contained longevity genes. Thereby, enabling knowledge to be maintained with in the family structure for centuries.

I am highly indebted to my mother whose sanity was very clear at the age of one hundred plus years of life. She provided driving directions to locations in Macon and Dooly Counties in Georgia from firsthand memory.

It was refreshing to confirm information provided by Luella and two of her sisters in U. S. decennial Census data, local maps of the area, obituaries, and cemetery records.

Various families' photo albums were used to provide images to enable readers to better relate to the many characters in this book.

The Internet was used as a resource for geographical data, maps, genealogy data, and quotes:

Geographical Historical Notes: http://maconcounty.georgia.gov/

Map of Macon County Georgia: http://georgia.gov/maconcounty

Map of the State of Georgia: http://georgia.gov
Quotes: http://www.all-famous-quotes.com
Lyrics: http://www.lyricsmania.com/
Newspapers: *Macon County Citizen*   *Cordele Dispatch*
The New National Baptist Hymnal, Copyright 1977, Tenth Edition

About the Author

Mary Beal was blessed and highly favored by the Lord to serve as Luella Campbell Beal's primary care giver from May 2005 until her death. Mary stated, "I received so many blessings that I cannot begin to jot them all down. However, by the grace of God there were more blessings than I can ever possibly recall". I hope that readers will find this book informative and inspiring. I also hope that readers' relationship with the Holy Spirit will increase based on Luella's personal experiences. Much of what has been written was derived from Mary's spiritual growth, guided by her intimate relationship with her mother and the Holy Spirit. Mary is a semi-retired federal government civil servant. Mary encourages her readers to look forward to the upcoming spiritual side of the Force to Reckon with in *Help Me Cross Over from Earth to Heaven*.

"All I am, or can be, I owe to my angel mother.".

Abraham Lincoln

www.ingramcontent.com/pod-product-compliance
Lightning Source LLC
Chambersburg PA
CBHW070500100426
42743CB00010B/1700